Poems by Thomas Gent

Thomas Gent was born in Ireland on 4th May 1693 and baptised as a Presbyterian.

In 1707 he was given an apprenticeship with Stephen Powell, a printer in Dublin. It turned out to be an unhappy time for Gent and in 1710 he took his leave and stowed away on a ship bound for England.

In London he obtained another printing apprenticeship under Edward Midwinter. After completing this in 1713, he worked briefly for a Mrs Bradford, and then a printer named Mears. Unsatisfied with his progress he turned to laboring for subsistence.

A few months later he obtained a post with John White, the King's printer for York. He also met here his future wife; Alice Guy.

By 1717 he was back in London and was admitted to the Company of Stationers, and also became a freeman of London.

He briefly returned to Ireland, visiting his parents, and then returned to London, taking up employment under a Roman Catholic named Clifton, and met Atterbury, Bishop of Rochester, for whom he then printed a defence of an imprisoned Clergyman.

Gent was requested by Midwinter on a number of occasions to return to work with him, and he eventually left the troublesome Clifton to rejoin him.

It was also now that Gent was briefly arrested, on suspicion of printing treasonable works, and placed in prison for five days, but was then released without charge.

His aim now was to establish himself as a printer in his own right, so that he might have the means to marry Alice. However, she had married Charles Bourne, grandson of John White and inheritor of his printshop, in 1721.

In 1724 Alice was widowed, and Gent travelled to York to once more attempt marriage. He was successful and they married in York Minster in December 1724, and, by this marriage, he also obtained the print business in York. Gent now became the publisher of Yorkshire's only newspaper, the Original York Courant, or Weekly Journal, previously the York Mercury.

Their union produced a child within the year but sadly the boy, Charles, died at a very young age in 1726.

John White Jnr, printer of Newcastle, the son of John White, who had failed to obtain the York Press for himself set up a rival business in York. This venal competition prompted Gent to begin writing his own works, and he published a history of York in 1730, followed by another on Ripon in 1733, and then one on Hull in 1735. Gent's paper ceased publication in 1728, and White's The York Courant became the predominant local paper.

In 1735 Gent began publication of a journal 'Miscellanea Curiosa', concerned with mathematical and other problems; the publication was not a success.

In 1741 Gent published a history of England, and with it a history of Rome in the second volume.

From the 1740s Gent's business went into decline, due to competition from John White Jnr., and other printers who had also set up in York. He lost the lease on his house and to his print premises in Stonegate in 1742. He and Alice then moved to a house in Petergate, where he continued to publish but with reduced output. From here he published several works covering religious topics, in poem form, the first being 'The Holy Life and Death of St. Winefred'.

On 1st April 1761 his wife, Alice died.

Gent's own circumstances were much reduced in the last decades of his life; he struggling with illness, and poverty, and had to rely on the charity of friends.

Thomas Gent died on 19th May 1778. He was buried at St. Michael-le-Belfry in York.

Index of Contents

ADVERTISEMENT

Some of the Pieces in this volume have been separately published, at different times; the indulgence, I may say favour, with which they were individually received, has encouraged me to collect and re-publish them. I have added many others, which are now first printed. I shall be well satisfied, if they find as favourable a reception as their precursors; and are thought not to have increased the size, without at all increasing the merit, of the book.

I cannot omit this opportunity of thanking those Critics, who have honoured me by reviewing my verses. I owe them my warm acknowledgments for candidly measuring my Poems by their pretensions. They have looked at them as they really were;—as the amusements of the leisure hours of a man whose fortune will not favour his inclination to devote himself to poetry; and conceiving a favourable opinion of them in that character, have kindly expressed it.

London, December, 1827.

During the progress of these pages through the press, it has pleased Providence to inflict upon me the severest calamity that domestic life can sustain. In the private sorrows of the humble candidate for literary fame, I am aware that the world will feel no interest, yet humanity will forgive the weakness that struggles under such a bereavement, and will pardon the tear that falls upon such a tomb. If, indeed, the Being who is lost to her family and society were endowed only with those gifts and graces, which are shared by thousands of her sex, I should have been silent at this moment. To those who knew her,[1] and to know her was to esteem and love, this tribute will be superfluous; but to those who knew her not, I would say, that, superadded to every natural advantage, to the charms of every polite accomplishment, and to a cheerful and sincere piety, she was deeply imbued with the love of literature and of science. In these, her Lectures on the Physiology of the External Senses exhibit a splendid proof of her acquirements in their highest walks, and are an imperishable memorial of her patient and laborious research. They who were present at the delivery of these Lectures will not soon forget the effect of her impressive elocution, chastened as it was by as unaffected modesty as ever adorned and dignified a woman. I speak of that which she performed—that which her capacious mind had meditated I forbear to mention. For the advancement of her sex in pursuits that are intellectual she made many sacrifices, both of her feelings and her time; yet, in all she did, and in all she contemplated, usefulness was her end and aim—but I must not proceed; less than this I could not say—more than this might be deemed ostentatious.

What earthly tongue, and, oh! what human pen
  Can tell that scene of suffering, too severe.
'Tis ever present to my sight, oh! when
  Will the sound cease its torture on mine ear?
Oh! my lost love, thou patient Being, never!
  Thy dying look of love can I forget;
The last fond pressure of thy hand, for ever!
  Thrills in my veins, I see thy struggles yet.
Thy sculptured beauty is before me now:
  In thy calm dignity, and sweet repose,
Alas! sad memory re-invests thy brow,
  With death's stern agony, and pain's last throes.
Desolate heart be still—forgive, oh God!
  The cries of feeble nature stricken sore.
Father! assuage the terrors of thy rod.
  Teach me to see thy wisdom—and adore!

[Footnote 1: I cannot resist the melancholy gratification of quoting from the Literary Gazette, of August 18, in which the death of Mrs. Gent was announced to the public.—"Science has, since our last, suffered a severe lost by the death of this accomplished lady; she was well known for her high attainments as a Lecturer, and her Course on the Physiology of the External Senses was a perfect model of elegant composition and refined oratory. Mrs. Gent died at the residence of her husband, Thomas Gent, Esq. Doctor's Commons, after a month of severe suffering, which she bore with singular fortitude, and the most pious resignation. There is a fine bust of her, by Behnes; it was in the Exhibition two years since, and, from its intrinsic simplicity and beauty alone, has had many casts made from it."

And one of the most distinguished Poets of the present day, will, I am sure, forgive me if I quote his beautiful words in writing to me on this subject—for his talents she had the highest admiration, and no one was better able than himself to appreciate the excellence of her character.—"As to condolence, I never condole—what condolence could any one offer for the loss of so estimable a being as has been lost to society in your accomplished wife? I had a very great respect and esteem for her, and it would have highly gratified me to have been able to lighten the least of her trials; but what avails writing or visiting on occasions of such real pain. She lived a most amiable being—and for such there is the highest hope in the Highest World. If I had conceived that her illness was at all serious, I should have gone to gather wisdom from her for my own hour—but now, that all her anxieties are past, I can invent no condolence."]

POEMS

Tis sweet in boyhood's visionary mood,
When glowing Fancy, innocently gay,
Flings forth, like motes, her bright aërial brood,
To dance and shine in Hope's prolific ray;

'Tis sweet, unweeting how the flight of years
May darkling roll in trials and in tears,
To dress the future in what garb we list,
And shape the thousand joys that never may exist.
But he, sad wight! of all that feverish train,
Fool'd by those phantoms of the wizard brain,
Most wildly dotes, whom young ambition stings
To trust his weight upon poetic wings;
He, downward looking in his airy ride,
Beholds Elysium bloom on every side;
Unearthly bliss each thrilling nerve attunes,
And thus the dreamer with himself communes.
Yes! Earth shall witness, 'ere my star be set,
That partial nature mark'd me for her pet;
That Phoebus doom'd me, kind indulgent sire!
To mount his car, and set the world on fire.
Fame's steep ascent by easy flights to win,
With a neat pocket volume I'll begin;
And dirge, and sonnet, ode, and epigram,
Shall show mankind how versatile I am.
The buskin'd Muse shall next my pen descry:
The boxes from their inmost rows shall sigh;
The pit shall weep, the galleries deplore
Such moving woes as ne'er were heard before:
Enough—I'll leave them in their soft hysterics,
Mount, in a brighter blaze, and dazzle with Homerics.
Then, while my name runs ringing through Reviews,
And maids, wives, widows, smitten with my Muse,
Assail me with Platonic billet-doux.
From this suburban attic I'll dismount,
With Coutts or Barclays open an account;
Ranged in my mirror, cards, with burnish'd ends,
Shall show the whole nobility my friends;
That happy host with whom I choose to dine,
Shall make set-parties, give his-choicest wine;
And age and infancy shall gape to see
The lucky bard, and whisper "That is he!"
Poor youth! he print—and wakes, to sleep no more—
The world goes on, indifferent, as before;
And the first notice of his metric skill
Comes in the likeness of—his printer's bill;
To pen soft notes no fair enthusiast stirs,
Except his laundress—and who values her's?
None but herself: for though the bard may burn
Her note, she still expects one in return.
The luckless maiden, all unblest shall sigh;
His pocket tome hath drawn his pockets dry.
His tragedy expires in peals of laughter;

And that soul-thrilling wish—to live hereafter—
Gives way to one as hopeless quite, I fear,
And far more needful—how to live while here.
Where are ye now, divine illusions all;
Cheques, dinners, wines, admirers great and small!
Changed to two followers, terrible to see,
Who dog his walks, and whisper "That is he!"
Rhymesters attend! nor scorn & friendly hint,
Restrain your cacoëths fierce to print.
But hark, my printer's devil's at the door,
My leisure cannot yield one moment more:
Nor matters it, advice can ne'er restrain
Madman or poet from his bent:—'tis vain
To strive to point out colours to the blind,
Or set men seeking what they will not find.

MATURE REFLECTIONS

O Love! divinest dream of youth,
  Thy day of ecstacy is o'er,
My bosom, touch'd by time and truth,
  Thrills at thy dear deceits no more.
Nor thou, Ambition! e'er again,
  With splendour dazzling to betray,
And aspirations fierce and vain,
  Shall tempt my steps—away! away!
Alas! by stern Experience cleft,
  When life's romance is turn'd to sport;
If man hath consolation left
  On this side death—'tis good old port.
And thou, Advice! who glum and chill,
  Do'st the third bottle still gainsay;
Smile, and partake it, if you will,
  But if you wont—away! away!

THE GRAVE OF DIBDIN

Lives there who, with unhallow'd hand, would tear,
One leaf from that immortal wreath which shades
The Hero's living brow, or decks his urn?
Breathes there who does not triumph in the thought
That "Nelson's language is his mother tongue,"
And that St. Vincent's country is his own?
Oh! these bright guerdons of renown are won

By means most palpable to sense and sight;
By days of peril and by nights of toil;
By Valour's long probation, closed at last
In Victory's arms—consummated and seal'd
In deathless Glory and immortal Fame.
Musing I stand upon his lowly grave,
Who, though he fought no battle—though he pour'd
No hostile thunders on his country's foes,
Achieved for Britain triumphs, less array'd
"In pomp and circumstance," nor visible
To vulgar gaze—the triumphs of the Mind.
He nursed the elements of courage—he
Supplied the aliment that feeds and guides
The daring spirit to its high emprise—
A nation's moral energies, by him
Directed, found a nobler end and aim.
He gave that high discriminating tone
That marks the Brave from mercenary tools—
Features that separate a British Crew
From hireling bravoes, and from pirate hordes.
And yet no marble marks the spot where lies
The dust of DIBDIN;—no inscription speaks
A Nation's gratitude—a Bard's desert.
The youthful Sailor on his midnight watch,
Fixing his gaze upon the tranquil moon,
Felt his heart soften as the thoughts of home
Rush'd on his faithful memory;—then it was
In language meet, and in appropriate strains—
Strains which thy lyre had taught him—he pour'd forth
The feelings of his soul, and all was calm.
Thy Spirit still presides in that carouse,
When to "the Far away" the toast is given,
And "absent Wives and Sweethearts" claim their right,
With Woman's constancy thy songs are rife;
And this pure creed still teaches Man t' endure
Privations, danger, and each form of death.
When not a breath responded to the call,
And Seamen whistled to the winds in vain;
When the loose canvass droop'd in lazy folds,
And idle pennants dangled from the mast;—
There, in that trying moment, thou wert found
To teach the hardest lesson man can learn—
Passive endurance—and the breeze has sprung,
As if obedient to the voice of Song:—
And yet unhonour'd here thy ashes lie!
A nobler lesson learn'd the gallant Tar
From his Orphean lyre—to temper right
The lion's courage with the attributes

That to the gentle and the meek belong;
O'er fallen foes to check the eye of fire—
O'er fallen foes to soften heart of oak.
He turn'd the Fatalist's rash eye to Him
In whom the issues are of life and death;
He taught to whom the battle is—to whom
The victory belongs. His cherub, that aloft
Kept sleepless watch, was Providence—not Chance.
And yet no honours are decreed for him—
Friend of the Brave, thy memory cannot die!
Th'inquiring voice, that eagerly demands
Where rest thy ashes?—shall preserve thy fame.
Thine immortality thyself hast wrought;—
Familiar as the terms of art, thy verse,
Thine own peculiar words are still the mode
In which the Seaman aptly would express
His honest passions and his manly thoughts;
His feelings kindle at thy burning words,
Which speak his duty in the battle's front;
His parting whisper to the maid he loves
Is breathed in eloquence he learned from thee;
Thou art his Oracle in every mood—
His trump of victory—his lyre of love!

A SKETCH FROM LIFE

She sat in beauty, like some form of nymph
Or naïad, on the mossy, purpled bank
Of her wild woodland stream, that at her feet
Linger'd, and play'd, and dimpled, as in love.
Or like those shapes that on the western clouds
Spread gold-dropp'd plumes, and sing to harps of pearl,
And teach the evening winds their melody:
How shall I tell her beauty?—for the eye,
Fix'd on the sun, is blinded by its beam.
One glance, and then no more, upon that brow
Brighter than marble shining through those curls,
Richer than hyacinths when they wave their bells
In the low breathing of the twilight wind.—
One glance upon that lip, beside whose hue
The morning rose would sicken and grow pale,
'Till it was waked again by the soft breath
That steals in music from those lips of love.
Wert thou a statue I could pine for thee,
But in thy living beauty there is awe;
The sacredness of modesty enshrines

The ruby lip, bright brow, and beaming eye;—
I dare but worship what I must not love.

ON THE PORTRAIT OF THE SON OF J.G. LAMBTON, ESQ., M.P. BY SIR THOMAS LAWRENCE, P.R.A.

Beautiful Boy—thy heavenward thoughts
  Are pictured in thine eyes,
Thou hast no taint of mortal birth,
Thy communing is not of earth,
  Thy holy musings rise:
Like incense kindled from on high,
Ascending to its native sky.
And such a head might once have graced
  The infant Samuel, when
Call'd by the favour of his God,
The youthful priest the Temple trod
  Beloved of Heaven and men!
The same devotion on his brow
As brightens in thy forehead now.
Or, thou may'st seem to Fancy's eye
  One borne by arms Divine;
One, whom on Earth a Saviour bless'd,
And on whose features left impress'd
  The Contact's holy sign:
A light, a halo, and a grace,
So pure th' expression of that face.
Or, has the Painter's skill alone
  Such grace and glory given?
Clothed thee with attributes which seem
Creations of an angel's dream,
  To raise the soul to Heaven?
No, as he found thee, he arrayed,
And Genius taught what God had made!

WRITTEN IN THE ALBUM OF THE LADY OF COUNSELLOR D. POLLOCK

Joy to thee, Lady! many years of joy
  To thee—and thine—that springtide of the heart,
The bliss of virtuous love, without alloy.
  And all that health and gladsome life impart.
How gracefully hast thou thy task perform'd,
  The watchful tender mother, matchless wife;
All woman boasts—thou hast indeed adorn'd—
  Thine the high merit of an useful life.

For ever cheerful, though the Tragic Muse[1]
  May call thee Sister, both in form and mind;
Thou do'st to all those envied charms transfuse,
  Which shine so highly temper'd and refined.
Lady revered—the sunbeam and the rose
  Are poor in beauty to sweet woman's smiles:
'Tis the bright sunset of life's awful close,
  The Poet's deathless wreath! a spell all grief beguiles!

[Footnote 1: The Lady, to whom these lines are addressed has been greatly noticed for the strong resemblance she bears to Mrs. Siddons.]

THE HELIOTROPE

There is a flower, whose modest eye
  Is turn'd with looks of light and love,
Who breathes her softest, sweetest sigh.
  Whene'er the sun is bright above.
Let clouds obscure, or darkness veil,
  Her fond idolatry is fled,
Her sighs no more their sweets exhale.
  The loving eye is cold—and dead.
Canst thou not trace a moral here,
  False flatterer of the prosperous hour?
Let but an adverse cloud appear,
  And Thou art faithless, as the Flower!

SONNET. ON SEEING A YOUNG LADY, I HAD PREVIOUSLY KNOWN, CONFINED IN A MADHOUSE

Sweet wreck of loveliness! alas, how soon
  The sad brief summer of thy joys hath fled:
How sorrows Friendship for thy hapless doom,
  Thy beauty faded, and thy hopes all dead.
Oh! 'twas that beauty's power which first destroy'd
  Thy mind's serenity; its charms but led
The faithless friend, that thy pure love enjoy'd,
  To tear the beauteous blossom from its bed.
How reason shudders at thy frenzied air!
  To see thee smile, with fancy's dreams possess'd;
Or shrink, the frozen image of despair.
  Or, love-enraptured, chant thy griefs to rest:
Oh! cease that mournful voice, affliction's child,
  My heart but bleeds to hear thy musings wild.

PROMETHEUS

What sovereign good shall satiate man's desires,
Propell'd by Hope's unconquerable fires?
Vain each bright bauble by ambition prized;
Unwon, 'tis worshipp'd—but possess'd, despised.
Yet all defect with virtue shines allied,
His mightiest impulse genius owes to pride.
From conquer'd science graced with glorious spoils,
He still dares on, demands sublimer toils;
And, had not Nature check'd his vent'rous wing,
His eye had pierced her at her primal spring.
Thus when, enwrapt, Prometheus strove to trace
Inspired perceptions of celestial grace,
Th' ideal spirit, fugitive as wind,
Art's forceful spells in adamant confined:
Curved with nice chisel floats the obsequious line;
From stone unconscious, beauty beams divine;
On magic poised, th' exulting structure swims,
And spurns attraction with elastic limbs.
While ravish'd fancy vivifies the form;
While judgment toils to analyze its charm;
While admiration spreads her speaking hands;
The lofty artist undelighted stands.
He longs to ravish from the bless'd abodes
The seal of heaven, the attribute of gods;
To give his labour more than man can give,
Breathe Jove's own breath, and bid the marble live!
Won from her woof, embellishing the skies,
Descending, Pallas soothes her vot'ry's sighs,
Where, 'midst the twilight of o'er-arching groves,
By waking visions led, th' enthusiast roves;
Like summer suns, by showery clouds conceal'd,
With sudden blaze the goddess shines reveal'd:
Behold, she cries, in thy distinguished cause
I challenge Jove's inexorable laws!
With life-stol'n essence let th' awaken'd stone
A super-human generation own.
Defrauded nature shall admire the deed,
And time recoil at thy immortal meed.
Impregn'd with action, and convoked to breathe,
Sighs the still form his ardent hands beneath;
Electric lustres flash from either eve,
O'er its pale cheeks suffusive flushes fly,
And glossy damps its clust'ring curls adorn,
Like dew-drops bright'ning on the brows of morn.

Through nerves that vibrate in unfolding chains,
Foams the warm life-blood, excavating veins;
'Till all infused, and organized the whole,
The finish'd fabric hails the breathing soul!
Then waked tumultuous in th' alarmed breast,
Contending passions claim th' etherial guest;
And still, as each alternate empire proves,
She hopes, she fears, she envies, and she loves;
Owns all sensations that deride the span,
And eternize the little life of man!

ROSA'S GRAVE

It is a mournful pleasure to remember the exquisite taste and delight she evinced in the arrangement of a Bouquet; and how often she wished that, hereafter, she might appear to me as a beautiful flower!

Oh! lay me where my Rosa lies,
  And love shall o'er the moss-grown bed,
When dew-drops leave the weeping skies.
  His tenderest tear of pity shed.
And sacred shall the willow be,
  That shades the spot where virtue sleeps;
And mournful memory weep to see
  The hallow'd watch affection keeps.
Yes, soul of love! this bleeding heart
  Scarce beating, soon its griefs shall cease;
Soon from his woes the sufferer part,
  And hail thee at the Throne of Peace

THE SIBYL. A SKETCH.

So stood the Sibyl: stream'd her hoary hair
Wild as the blast, and with a comet's glare
Glow'd her red eye-balls 'midst the sunken gloom
Of their wild orbs, like death-fires in a tomb.
Slow, like the rising storm, in fitful moans,
Broke from her breast the deep prophetic tones.
Anon, with whirlwind rash, the Spirit came;
Then in dire splendour, like imprison'd flame
Flashing through rifted domes or towns amazed,
Her voice in thunder burst; her arm she raised;
Outstretch'd her hands, as with a Fury's force,
To grasp, and launch the slow descending curse:
Still as she spoke, her stature seem'd to grow;

Still she denounced unmitigable woe:
Pain, want, and madness, pestilence, and death,
Rode forth triumphant at her blasting breath:
Their march she marshall'd, taught their ire to fall—
And seem'd herself the emblem of them all!

LOVE

Love!—what is love? a mere machine, a spring
For freaks fantastic, a convenient thing,
A point to which each scribbling wight most steer,
Or vainly hope for food or favour here;
A summer's sigh; a winter's wistful tale:
A sound at which th' untutor'd maid turns pale;
Her soft eyes languish, and her bosom heaves,
And Hope delights as Fancy's dream deceives.
Thus speaks the heart which cold disgust invades,
When time instructs, and Hope's enchantment fades;
Through life's wide stage, from sages down to kings,
The puppets move, as art directs the strings:
Imperious beauty bows to sordid gold,
Her smiles, whence heaven flows emanent, are sold;
And affectation swells th' entrancing tones,
Which nature subjugates, and truth disowns.
I love th' ingenuous maiden, practised not
To pierce the heart with ambush'd glances, shot
From eyelashes, whose shadowy length she knows
To a hair's point, their high arch when to close
Half o'er the swimming orb, and when to raise,
Disclosing all the artificial blaze
Of unfelt passion, which alone can move
Him whom the genuine eloquence of love
Affected never, won with wanton wiles,
With soulless sighs, and meretricious smiles;
By nature unimpress'd, uncharm'd by thee,
Sweet goddess of my heart, Simplicity!

ON A DELIGHTFUL DRAWING IN MY ALBUM, By my friend, T. WOODWARD, ESQ., of a Group, consisting of a Donkey, a Boy, and a Dog

Welcome, my pretty Neddy—welcome too
Thy merry Rider with his apron blue;
And thou, poor Dog, most patient thing of all,
Begging for morsels that may never fall!

Oh! 'tis a faithful group—and it might shame
Painters of bold pretence, and greater name—
To see how nature triumphs, and how rare
Such matchless proofs of Nature's triumphs are—
The smallest particle of sand may tell
With what rich ore Pactolus' tide may swell:
And Woodward! this ingenious, chaste design,
Proclaims what treasures lie within the mine—
Pupil of Cooper—Nature's favorite son—
Whom, but to name, and to admire, is one!

STANZAS

Say, why is the stern eye averted with scorn
  Of the stoic who passes along?
And why frowns the maid, else as mild as the morn.
  On the victim of falsehood and wrong?
For the wretch sunk in sorrow, repentance, and shame,
  The tear of compassion is won:
And alone must she forfeit the wretch's sad claim,
  Because she's deceived and undone?
Oh! recal the stern look, ere it reaches her heart,
  To bid its wounds rankle anew;
Oh! smile, or embalm with a tear the sad smart,
  And angels will smile upon you.
Time was, when she knew nor opprobrium nor pain,
  And youth could its pleasures impart,
Till some serpent distill'd through her bosom the stain,
  As he wound round the strings of her heart.
Poor girl! let thy tears through thy blandishments break,
  Nor strive to retrace them within;
For mine would I mingle with those on thy cheek,
  Nor think that such sorrow were sin.
When the low-trampled reed, and the pine in its pride,
  Shall alike feel the hand of decay,
May thy God grant that mercy the world has denied,
  And wipe all your sorrows away!

SHAKSPEARE

Respectfully inscribed, with permission, to the Committee (of which His Majesty is the Patron) for the proposed Monuments to SHAKSPEARE at Stratford and in London. Intended to be spoken at one of the Theatres.

While o'er this pageant of sublunar things
Oblivion spreads her unrelenting wings,
And sweeps adown her dark unebbing tide
Man, and his mightiest monuments of pride—
Alone, aloft, immutable, sublime,
Star-like, ensphered above the track of time,
Great SHAKSPEARE beams with undiminish'd ray.
His bright creations sacred from decay,
Like Nature's self, whose living form he drew,
Though still the same, still beautiful and new.
He came, untaught in academic bowers,
A gift to Glory from the Sylvan powers:
But what keen Sage, with all the science fraught,
By elder bards or later critics taught,
Shall count the cords of his mellifluous shell,
Span the vast fabric of his fame, and tell
By what strange arts he bade the structure rise—
On what deep site the strong foundation lies?
This, why should scholiasts labour to reveal?
We all can answer it, we all can feel,
Ten thousand sympathies, attesting, start—
For SHAKSPEARE'S Temple, is the human heart!
Lord of a throne which mortal ne'er shall share—
Despot adored! he rales and revels there.
Who but has found, where'er his track hath been,
Through life's oft shifting, multifarious scene,
Still at his side the genial Bard attend,
His loved companion, counsellor, and friend!
The Thespian Sisters nurtured in the schools
Of Greece and Rome, and long coerced by rules,
Scarce moved the inmates of their native hearth
With tiny pathos and with trivial mirth,
Till She, great muse of daring enterprise,
Delighted ENGLAND! saw her SHAKSPEARE rise!
Then, first aroused in that appointed hour,
The Tragic Muse confess'd th' inspiring power;
Sudden before the startled earth she stood,
A giant spectre, weeping tears and blood;
Guilt shrunk appall'd, Despair embraced his shroud,
And Terror shriek'd, and Pity sobb'd aloud;—
Then, first Thalia with dilated ken
And quicken'd footstep pierced the walks of men;
Then Folly blush'd, Vice fled the general hiss,
Delight met Reason with a loving kiss;
At Satire's glance Pride smooth'd his low'ring crest,
The Graces weaved the dance.—And last and best
Came Momus down in Falstaff's form to earth.
To make the world one universe of mirth!

Such Sympathies the glorious Bard endear!
Thus fair he walks in Man's diurnal sphere.
But when, upborne on bright Invention's wings.
He dares the realms of uncreated things,
Forms more divine, more dreadful, start to view,
Than ever Hades or Olympus knew.
Round the dark cauldron, terrible and fell,
The midnight Witches breathe the songs of hell;
Delighted Ariel wings his fiery way
To whirl the storm, the wheeling Orbs to stay;
Then bathes in honey-dews, and sleeps in flowers;
Meanwhile, young Oberon, girt with shadowy powers,
Pursues o'er Ocean's verge the pale cold Moon,
Or hymns her, riding in her highest noon.
Thus graced, thus glorified, shall SHAKSPEARE crave
The Sculptor's skill, the pageant of the grave?
HE needs it not—but Gratitude demands
This votive offering at his Country's hands.
Haply, e'er now, from blissful bowers on high,
From some Parnassus of the empyreal sky,
Pleased, o'er this dome the gentle Spirit bends,
Accepts the gift, and hails us as his friends—
Yet smiles, perchance, to think when envious Time
O'er Bust and Urn shall bid his ivies climb,
When Palaces and Pyramids shall fall—
HIS PAGE SHALL TRIUMPH—still surviving all—
'Till Earth itself, "like breath upon the wind,"
Shall melt away, "nor leave a rack behind!"

IMPROMPTU, TO ORIANA

ON ATTENDING WITH HER, AS SPONSORS, AT A CHRISTENING

Lady! who didst—with angel-look and smile,
And the sweet lustre of those dear, dark eyes,
Gracefully bend before the font of Christ,
In humble adoration, faith, and prayer!
Oh!—as the infant pledge of friends beloved
Received from thy pure lips its future name,
Sweetly unconscious look'd the baby-boy!
How beautifully helpless—and how mild!
—Methought, a seraph spread her shelt'ring wings
Over the solemn scene; and as the sun,
In its full splendour, on the altar came,
God's blessing seem'd to sanctify the deed.

TO MY SPANIEL FANNY

Fanny! were all the world like thee,
  How cheerly then this life would glide,
Dear emblem of Fidelity!
  Long may'st thou grace thy master's side.
Long cheer his hours of solitude,
  With watchful eye each wish to learn,
And anxious speechless gratitude
  Hail with delight each short sojourn.
When sick at heart, thy welcome home
  A weary load of grief dispels,
Gladdens with hope the hours to come,
  And yet a mournful lesson tells!
To find thee ever faithful, kind,
  My guard by night, my friend by day,
While those in friendship more refined
  Have with my fortunes flown away.
Why bounteous nature hast thou given
  To this poor Brute—a boon so kind
As constancy—bless'd gift of Heaven!
  And MAN—to waver like the wind?

WIDOWED LOVE [1]

Tell me, chaste spirit! in yon orb of light,
  Which seems to wearied souls an ark of rest,
So calm, so peaceful, so divinely bright—
  Solace of broken hearts, the mansion of the bless'd!
Tell me, oh! tell me—shall I meet again
  The long lost object of my only love!
—This hope but mine, death were release from pain;
  Angel of mercy! haste, and waft my soul above!

[Footnote 1: Mr. T. Millar has composed sweet music to these lines, and has been peculiarly fortunate in composing and singing some of the exquisite Melodies of T.H. Bayly, Esq. of Bath.]

WRITTEN IN THE ALBUM OF THE LADY OF DR. GEORGE BIRKBECK, M.D.

President of the London Mechanic's Institution, and of the Chemical and Meteorological Societies. Founder and Patron of the Glasgow Mechanic's Institute, &c. &c. &c.

Lady unknown! a pilgrim from the shrine
Of Poesy's fair temple, brings a wreath
Which fame and gratitude alike entwine,
Around a name that charms the monster Death,
And bids him pause!—Amidst despairing life
BIRKBECK's the harbinger of hope and health;
When sordid affluence was with man at strife,
He boldly stripp'd the veil, and show'd the wealth
To aged ignorance, and ardent youth,
Of cultured minds—the freedom of the soul!
The sun of science, and the light of truth,
The bliss of reason—mind without control.
Accept this tribute. Lady! and the praise,
As Consort and the soother of his care!
His offspring's pride—his friend's commingled rays,
And every other grace that man has deem'd most rare!

THE CHAIN-PIER, BRIGHTON; A SKETCH

Hail, lovely morn! and thou, all-beauteous sea!
Sun-sparkling with the diamond's countless rays:
Thy look, how tranquil, one eternal calm,
Which seems to woo the troubled soul to peace!
Now, all is sunshine, and thy boundless breast
Scarce heaves; unruffled, all thy waves subside
(Light murmuring, like the baby sighs of rest)
Into a gentle ripple on the shore.
All hail, dear Woman! saving-ark of man,
His surest solace in this world of woe;
How cheering are thy smiles, which, like the breeze
Of health, play softly o'er the pallid cheek,
And turn its rigid markings to a smile.
England may well be proud of scenes like this;
The beaming Beauty which adorns the PIER!
Hung like a fairy fabric o'er the sea,
The graceful wonder of this wondrous age;
Intrepid Brown,[1] the future page shall tell
Thy generous spirit's persevering aim,
That wrought so much, so well, thy country's weal;
How fit for thee, the gallant seaman's life,
His restless nights, and days of ceaseless toil;
Framed by thy mighty hand, the giant work
Check'd the rude tempest, in its fearful way.
Thy bold inventions gave new life to hope,
Steadied the wavering, and confirm'd the brave,
And bade the timid smile, amidst the storm!

Spirit of Hogarth! had I but one ray
Of that vast sun which warm'd thy varied mind;
How would I now describe the motley groups
Which crowd, in thoughtless ease, thy moving road.
Mark the young Confidence of yesterday,
Offspring of pride, and fortune's blinded fool,
(Engender'd like the vermin of an hour)
All would-be fashion, elegance, and ease,
While, by his side, the weaker vessel smirks,
In tawdry finery, with presuming gait,
As though the world were made for them alone;
Their liveried Lacquey, half-conceal'd in lace,
The vulgar wonder of an upstart race.
How heartlessly they pass that mourner by,
The poor lone Widow, with her death-struck load.
In speechless poverty, she courts the air,
To give its blessing to her suff'ring babe;
Not asking it herself; for life, to her,
Has now no charm—her refuge is the grave!
Here comes the moral Almanack of years—
The prim old maid, and, by her side, her Niece,
Full of bewitching beauty, health, and love.
See, how the tabby watches Laura's eyes,
Lest they should smile upon some pleasing spark,
And violate grim prudery's tyrant ties.
With icy finger, she her charge directs,
To view the faithful dial of the sun,
Whose moral tells how tide and time pass on.
See, there—the fated victim of mischance;
Read, in that hollow eye, and alter'd look,
The deep anxiety which gnaws the heart,
Incessant struggling 'gainst a tide of care,
Which wears his life away;—and there, again,
The empty, lucky Fool, who never thought,
Nor ever will, yet lives and smiles, and thrives!
Mark ye, that Ready-reckoner's figured face?
Cold calculation in his thoughtful step;
The heartless wretch, who never trusts his land,
And never is deceived!—And, next him, comes
Laughing Good-nature, with ruddy cheeks,
And welcome look, determined to be pleased.
He comes to ask—or go with friend to dine;
His labour but to dress—to eat, to sleep:
He knows no suffering equal to bad wine.
There—the prig-Parson, with indented hat,
And formal step—demanding your respect—
Yonder, the lovely insect-chasing Child.
His is, indeed, a life of envious joy;

Hope and anticipation, on the wing,
To him no sad realities e'er bring!
And now, the humble Quaker, plain and proud.
Humility, is this, indeed, thy type?
(I know it is not, for I know the man.)
His lovely Daughter bears an angel form
And mind, that glorifies her sex's charms;
Meekness and charity her life employ—
A seraph sorrowing for a suffering world!
Lo! too, the Matron, with her household gods,
The deities she worships night and day.
Affection has no bounds, nor language words.
To tell a mother's tender ceaseless charge.
Children! can all your future lore repay
The nights of watchfulness, and days of care,
Which a fond parent gives?—
See, last, sad sight! the hardy British Tar,
Cutlass unsheath'd, unlike the truly brave.
Here, watching, night and day—degenerate lot!
To seize a fisherman, or stop a cart,
Or "fright the wandering spirits from the shore."
His "brief authority" has just detain'd
A boat of cockles and a quart of gin!
The smart Lieutenant's epaulette, methinks,
Blushes at this degrading, pimping trade.—
For deeds like these—let objects be employ'd,
Who never shared their country's high renown!
Adieu! vast Ocean, cradle of the brave,
Tablet of England's glory, and her shield!
To thee—and those dear friends who lured me here,
With hospitality's enchanting smile,
And chased away a little age of woe—
Gratefully—I dedicate these tuneful lays!

July, 1826.

[Footnote 1: *My friend, Captain Samuel Brown, of the Royal Navy, whose inventions and improvements of the iron chain cable, and various others connected with the naval service, deserve the gratitude of his country, independent of the admirable Chain-Pier at Brighton, a Suspension Bridge over the Tweed, Pier at Newhaven, Bridge at Heckham, the iron work for Hammersmith Suspension Bridge, and other successful undertakings.*]

SONNET

MORNING

Light as the breeze that hails the infant morn
  The Milkmaid trips, as o'er her arm she slings
  Her cleanly pail, some fav'rite lay she sings
As sweetly wild and cheerful as the horn.
O! happy girl I may never faithless love,
  Or fancied splendour, lead thy steps astray;
  No cares becloud the sunshine of thy day,
Nor want e'er urge thee from thy cot to rove.
What though thy station dooms thee to be poor,
  And by the hard-earn'd morsel thou art fed;
  Yet sweet content bedecks thy lowly bed,
And health and peace sit smiling at thy door:
Of these possess'd—thou hast a gracious meed,
Which Heaven's high wisdom gives, to make thee rich indeed!

ON THE DEATH OF DR. ABEL [1]

Physician and Naturalist to Lord Amherst, Governor General of India, who died at Cawnpoor, 24th of November, 1826.

Another awful warning voice of death
To human dignity, and human pride;
'Tis sad, to mark how short the longest life—
How brief was thine! Thy day is done,
And all its complicated hopes and fears
Lie buried, ABEL! in an early grave.
The unavailing tear for thee shall flow,
And love and friendship faithful record keep
Of all thy varied worth, thy anxious strife
For fame and years, now gone for ever!
Yet o'er thy tomb science and learning
Bend in mute regret, and truth proclaims
Thy just inheritance an honour'd name!
Lamented most by those who knew thee best,
Accept this humble, tributary lay,
From one, who in thy boyhood and thy prime
Had shared thy friendship, and had fondly hoped
When last we parted, many years were thine
And joys in store—that thy elastic mind
Might long have gladden'd life's monotony.
Thine was a princely heart, a joyous soul,
The charm of reason, and the sprightly wit
Which kept dull letter'd ignorance in awe,
Shook the pretender on his tinsel throne,
And claim'd the glorious dignity of mind!
Alas! that in thy prime, when time began

To make thee nearly all the World could wish,
The spoiler Death should unrelenting come
(As though in envy of thy wondrous skill)
And stop the fountain of a noble heart.
Rest, anxious spirit! from life's feverish dream,
From all its sad realities and cares:
Be this thy Epitaph, thy honour'd boast—
Thine was the fame, which thine own mind achieved!

[Footnote 1: Dr. Abel was greatly distinguished in his profession for his love of it, and for the ardour of his pursuits in useful knowledge. —He published many ingenious Papers on Medical Science and Natural History. His account of the Embassy to China, under Lord Amherst, has been generally admired. He practised with increasing respect as a Physician, at Brighton, previous to his leaving England for India; and meditated (as the Author of this article knows) one or two works, which, from the activity of his mind, may yet be anticipated. Dr. Abel was a native of Bungay, in Suffolk (where his father was a banker), and it is supposed was about 35 years of age when he died. It is worthy of remark, that the present eminent and estimable Dr. Gooch, Librarian to His Majesty, and Dr. Abel, should both have been pupils of Mr. Borrett, Surgeon, of Yarmouth.]

SONNET

NIGHT

Now when dun Night her shadowy veil has spread,
  See want and infamy, as forth they come,
  Lead their wan daughter from her branded home,
To woo the stranger for unhallow'd bread.
Poor outcast! o'er thy sickly-tinted cheek
  And half-clad form, what havoc want hath made;
  And the sweet lustre of thine eye doth fade,
And all thy soul's sad sorrow seems to speak.
O! miserable state! compell'd to wear
  The wooing smile, as on thy aching breast
  Some wretch reclines, who feeling ne'er possess'd;
Thy poor heart bursting with the stifled tear!
Oh! GOD OF MERCY! bid her woes subside,
And be to her a friend, who hath no friend beside.

CONSTANCY

TO —.

Dearest love! when thy God shall recall thee,
  Be this record inscribed on thy tomb:

Truth, and gratitude, well may applaud thee,
  And all thy past virtues relume.
It shall tell—to thy sex's proud honour,
  Of sufferings and trials severe,
While still, through protracted affliction,
  Not a murmur escaped; but the tear
Of resignment to Heaven's high dictates,
  'Twas thine, like a martyr, to shed:
That heart—all affection for others—
  For thyself, uncomplainingly, bled.
Midst the storms, which misfortune had gather'd,
  What an angel thou wert unto me;
In that hour, when all friendship seem'd sever'd,
  Thou didst bloom like the ever-green tree!
All was gloom; and in vain had I striven,
  For hope ceased a ray to impart;
When thou cam'st, like a meteor from heaven,
  And gave peace to my desolate heart!

EPISTLE TO A FRIEND

Give me the wreath of friendship true,
  Whose flowerets fade not in a breath:
From memory gaining many a hue,
  To bloom beyond the touch of death.
And I will send it to thy home—
  Thy home beloved, my faithful friend!
And pray for its perpetual bloom
  And every bliss that earth can send.
Within its magic wreath I'd place
  Hearts'-ease and every lovely flower;
To win thee by their matchless grace,
  And cheer and bless the lonely hour.
When at the world's unkind return
  Of all thy worth, and all thy care,
Thou may'st in spite of manhood turn,
  And shed the sad, the bitter, tear.
Then, midst this holy grief of thine,
  The thought of some true friend may bless,
And cheer the gloom like angel's smile,
  Or sunbeam in a wilderness.
And could I hope I had a claim
  On thee in such a rapturous hour?
Oh! that, indeed, I'd own were fame.
  The saving ark of friendship's power.
Or that, in future years, thy babes

Should o'er this frail memorial bend,
(For first affection rarely fades!)
  And boast that I was once the friend
Whose wit, or worth, possess'd a charm,
  By Parents loved, and them caress'd.
That spell would every sorrow calm,
  And bid my anxious spirit rest!

HERE IN OUR FAIRY BOWERS WE DWELL

A GLEE

Sung by Messrs. GOULDEN, PYNE, and NELSON.—Composed by Mr. ROOKE

Here, in our fairy bowers, we dwell,
  Women our idol, life's best treasure!
Echo enchanted joys to tell,
  Our feast of laugh, of love, and pleasure.
      Say, is not this then bliss divine,
      Beauty's smiles and rosy wine?
Eternal mirth and sunshine reign,
  For grief we cannot find the leisure;
Night's social gods have banish'd pain,
  Morn lights us to increasing pleasure.
      Say, is not this then bliss divine,
      Beauty's smiles and rosy wine?
          Here in our fairy bowers, &c.

HENRY AND ELIZA

O'er the wide heath now moon-tide horrors hung,
  And night's dark pencil dimm'd the tints of spring;
The boding minstrel now harsh omens sung,
  And the bat spread his dark nocturnal wing.
At that still hour, pale Cynthia oft had seen
  The fair Eliza (joyous once and gay),
With pensive step, and melancholy mien,
  O'er the broad plain in love-born anguish stray.
Long had her heart with Henry's been entwined,
  And love's soft voice had waked the sacred blaze
Of Hymen's altar; while, with him combined,
  His cherub train prepared the torch to raise:
When, lo! his standard raging war uprear'd,
  And honour call'd her Henry from her charms.

He fought, but ah! torn, mangled, blood-besmear'd,
  Fell, nobly fell, amid his conquering arms!
In her sad bosom, a tumultuous world
  Of hopes and fears on his dear mem'ry spread;
For fate had not the clouded roll unfurl'd,
  Nor yet with baleful hemlock crown'd her head.
Reflection, oft to sad remembrance brought
  The well known spot, where they so oft had stray'd;
While fond affection ten-fold ardour caught,
  And smiling innocence around them play'd.
But these were past! and now the distant bell
  (For deep and pensive thought had held her there)
Toll'd midnight out, with long resounding knell,
  While dismal echoes quiver'd in the air.
Again 'twas silence—when from out the gloom
  She saw, with awe-struck eye, a phantom glide:
'Twas Henry's form!—what pencil shall presume
  To paint her horror!——HENRY AS HE DIED!
Enervate, long she stood—a sculptured dread,
  Till waking sense dissolved amazement's chain;
Then home, with timid haste, distracted fled,
  And sunk in dreadful agony of pain.
Not the deep sigh, which madden'd Sappho gave,
  When from Leucate's craggy height she sprung,
Could equal that which gave her to the grave,
  The last sad sound that echo'd from her tongue.

WRITTEN ON THE DEATH OF GENERAL WASHINGTON

Lamented Chief! at thy distinguish'd deeds
  The world shall gaze with wonder and applause,
While, on fair History's page, the patriot reads
  Thy matchless virtue in thy Country's cause.
Yes, it was thine, amid destructive war,
  To shield it nobly from oppression's chain;
By justice arm'd, to brave each threat'ning jar,
  Assert its freedom, and its rights maintain.
Much honour'd Statesman, Husband, Father, Friend,
  A generous nation's grateful tears are thine;
E'en unborn ages shall thy worth commend,
  And never-fading laurels deck thy shrine.
Illustrious Warrior! on the immortal base,
  By Freedom rear'd, thy envied name shall stand;
And Fame, by Truth inspired, shall fondly trace
  Thee, Pride and Guardian of thy Native Land!

To —.

In vain, sweet Maid! for me you bring
The first-blown blossoms of the spring;
My tearful cheek you wipe in vain,
And bid its pale rose bloom again.
In vain! unconscious, did I say?
Oh! you alone these tears can stay;
Alone, the pale rose can renew,
Whose sunshine is a smile from you.
Yet not in friendship's smile it lives;
Too cold the gifts that friendship gives:
The beam that warms a winter's day,
Plays coldly in the lap of May.
You bid my sad heart cease to swell,
But will you, if its tale I tell,
Nor turn away, nor frown the while,
But smile, as you were wont to smile?
Then bring me not the blossoms young,
That erst on Flora's forehead hung;
But round thy radiant temples twine,
The flowers whose flaunting mocks at mine.
Give me—nor pinks, nor pansies gay,
Nor violets, fading fast away,
Nor myrtle, rue, nor rosemary,
But give, oh! give, thyself to me!

MONODY TO THE MEMORY OF THE RIGHT HONOURABLE RICHARD BRINSLEY SHERIDAN

PREFACE TO SECOND EDITION

The very flattering success which attended the first Edition of this brief but affectionate Sketch, I must attribute to the interest of the subject, rather than the merit of the composition; and I cannot but feel grateful to those Writers who have honoured me by their notice and approbation.

I must not again go to press, without acknowledging how much I am indebted to a kind friend, who happened to be in Norfolk at the time I was printing the first Edition; with whom I had the happiness to pass many delightful hours, and to whose admirable taste and judgment I owe many valuable suggestions. In mentioning John Kemble with Sheridan, I associate two of the brightest stars that have illumined the Literature and Drama of the Country.

T.G.
Yarmouth, Norfolk, 1816.

SHERIDAN

Embalm'd in fame, and sacred from decay,
  What mighty name, in arms, in arts, or verse,
From England claims this consecrated day.
  Her nobles crowding round the shadowy hearse?
Hark! from yon fane, within whose hallow'd mounds,
  Her bards, her warriors, and her statesmen, sleep;
The solemn, slow, funereal bell resounds,
  While mournful echoes dread accordance keep.
Spirits revered! beyond that awful bourne.
  Who share the dark communion of the tomb,
A kindred genius seeks your dread sojourn;
  Ye heirs of glory! hail a brother home.
Obscured, as SHERIDAN to dust descends,
  Recedes each ray from Wit's effulgent sphere;
Lo! every Muse in silent sorrow bends,
  Her votive laurels mingling o'er his bier.
But chiefly thou, from whose polluted shrine
  His filial hand Circean rabble drove;
What pangs, Thalia! in this hour are thine;
  What fervent anguish of maternal love!
How long perverted, had the Comic scene,
  (The flattering reflex of a sensual age)
Shown prurient Folly's rank licentious mien,
  Refined, embellish'd on the pander stage:
While Vanburgh, Congreve, Farquhar, heaven-endow'd,
  To scourge bold Vice with Wit's resistless rod,
Embraced her chains, stood forth her priests avow'd,
  And scatter'd flowers in every path she trod:
Inglorious praise! though Judgment's self admired
  Those wanton strains which Virtue blush'd to hear;
While pamper'd Passion from the scene retired,
  With wilder rage to urge his fierce career.
At length, all graced in Fancy's orient hues,
  His native fires with added culture bright,
Rose SHERIDAN! to vindicate the Muse,
  And gild the drama with meridian light.
Him, skill'd alike great Nature's genuine form,
  Or Fashion's light factitious traits to trace,
The scene confess'd;—with glowing pathos warm,
  Or gaily sportive in familiar grace.
With what nice art his master-hand he flung
  O'er each fine chord which thrills the polish'd breast,
Let Faukland tell! with woes ideal stung;
  Let gentle Julia's generous flame attest![1]
Satire, that oft with castigation rude

Degrades, while zealous to correct mankind,
  Refined by him, more generous aims pursued,
  Reform'd the vice—but left no sting behind.
Yet, though with Wit's imperishable bays
  Enwreath'd, he held an uncontested throne;
Though circling climes, unanimous in praise,
  Confirm'd the partial suffrage of his own:
In careless mood he sought the Muse's bower;
  His lyre, like that to great Pelides strong,
The soft'ning solace of a vacant boor,
  Its airy descant indolently rung.
But when, portentous 'mid the storms of war,
  Glared Public danger; when, with withering din,
The spoil-flush'd foe strode furious from afar;
  And direr dread! Rebellion raged within:
Then SHERIDAN! dilating to the storm,
  Bright as the pharos, as the watch-tower strong,
With all the patriot's inspiration warm,
  Thy genius pour'd its thundering voice along.
Who heard thee not, in that tremendous hour,
  When Britain mourn'd her surest anchor lost,
And saw her alienated Navies lour,
  Like the charged tempest, round their parent coast?
With active zeal, which no cold medium knew,
  Nor party ruled, nor prejudice confined,
But, to thy heart's spontaneous impulse true,
  Thou gav'st thy country ALL thy mighty mind.
What time Iberia, gash'd with many a scar,
  Braved the fierce Gaul, in fervour uncontroll'd,
Though doubts and fears bedimm'd her struggling star,
  Its bright ascent thy prescient soul foretold.
Late, too, when France, with sophist cunning fraught,
  Essay'd that field which force had fail'd to gain,
And proudly question'd, by success untaught,
  Britannia's lineal right—her watery reign!
While meaner foes denounced with equal hate
  Her flag, which wide in Freedom's cause unfurl'd,
The saving sign of many a sinking state,
  Had chased Oppression from th' insulted world.—
Oh! that beyond the light diurnal page,
  Inscribed on high in monumental gold,
That strain might kindle each succeeding age,
  Which thus thy generous indignation roll'd:
"If e'er, of ancient energy bereaved,
  Britannia, bent by menace or design,
Should stain her naval sceptre, hard-achieved,
  And yield one claim, one cherish'd right resign:
"Then, hurl'd in ruin from her radiant sphere,

Sunk her proud Isle in Ocean's depths profound;
May all her glories pass from Memory's ear,
  An idle legend—a derided sound!"
Such were his merits whom the Muse deplores,
  The Wit, the Statesman, Orator, and Bard!
Nor when his frailties jealous truth explores,
  Shall Candour shrink from her supreme award?
If, all propitious, when his ardent prime
  Beat high with hope, in conscious powers elate,
Ambition woo'd him from her height sublime,
  And partial Fortune op'd her golden gate;
What hostile influence, glooming o'er his way,
  Chill'd each fine impulse, each aspiring aim,
Effused bleak clouds round Life's declining ray,
  And left his labours no reward but fame?
'Twas not alone that in the festive bower,
  Prompt in the social sympathies to melt,
Too long he linger'd; that the genial hour
  His fervid sense too exquisitely felt.
But that in tasks of public duty proved,
  Onward with faith inflexible he trod;
Alike by Fortune's dazzling lure unmoved,
  Or stern Necessity's relentless rod.
E'en Envy's self shall sanction that applause:
  And oft, slow pacing yon sepulchral gloom,
With fond regret shall Meditation pause,
  And breathe these accents o'er his honour'd tomb:
Ye Muses! come, with ministry divine.
  Protect the shrine where SHERIDAN is laid;
Ye Patriot Virtues! here your homage join;
  Assert his worth, and soothe his hovering shade.
Emblazon'd high in Albion's rolls of fame,
  A guiding star by which her sons may steer;
This proud inscription let his memory claim—
  Above himself, he held his Country dear!

[Footnote 1: Rivals.]

ON THE BEAUTIFUL PORTRAIT OF MRS. FOREMAN, AS PANDORA

In the Somerset-house Exhibition, 1826.—Painted by J.P. Davis

Oh! had'st thou, Jove! with adamantine locks
Fix'd fast the springs of poor Pandora's box,
Then had she, bright enchantment! bloom'd for ever
In all the charms consenting Gods could give her—
Wit, Wisdom, Beauty, she had every grace

Which makes man play the madman for a face!
But chief, bless'd gift! for him ordain'd to ask it,
The gem of gems, th' incomparable casket;
And, lo! with trembling hands and ardent eyes
The bridegroom claims it—and—behold the prize!
First, like a vapour o'er the heavens obscured,
From that dark confine, rose the fiends immured,
Then groan'd the earth, in fury swell'd the floods,
Blasts smote the harvests, lightning fired the woods;
Blue spotted Plague rode gibbering on the blast,
And nations shriek'd, and perish'd, as he pass'd.
Amazed, indignant, Epimetheus stood,
Vow'd dire revenge, and strung his nerves for blood.
It was not then, that from the coffer's lid
Hope's roseate smile his fierce delirium chid;
He saw, in that fair wife which heaven had sent
But mighty Mischiefs mortal instrument,
And swore not Hope, nor Mercy's self should save her,
Look'd in her face, smiled, sigh'd, and then—forgave her!

SONNET TO —, ON HER RECOVERY FROM ILLNESS

Fair flower! that fall'n beneath the angry blast,
Which marks with wither'd sweets its fearful way,
I grieve to see thee on the low earth cast,
While beauty's trembling tints fade fast away.
But who is she, that from the mountain's head
Comes gaily on, cheering the child of earth?
The walks of woe bloom bright beneath her tread,
And Nature smiles with renovated mirth?
'Tis Health! She comes: and, hark! the vallies ring,
And, hark! the echoing hills repeat the sound:
She sheds the new-blown blossoms of the spring,
And all their fragrance floats her footsteps round.
And, hark! she whispers in the zephyr's voice,
Lift up thy head, fair floweret, and rejoice!

THE RUNAWAY

Ah! who is he by Cynthia's gleam
 Discern'd, the statue of distress;
Weeping beside the willow'd stream
 That laves the woodland wilderness?
Why talks he to the idle air?

Why, listless, at his length reclined,
Heaves he the groan of deep despair,
  Responsive of the midnight wind?
Speak, gentle shepherd! tell me why?
  —Sir! he has lost his wife, they say:—
Of what disorder did, she die?
  —Lord, sir! of none—she ran away.

TO MARGARET JANE H—, ON HER BIRTH-DAY, 17 JUNE

Thou art indeed a lovely flower,
And I, just like the fleeting hour,
Which few will heed on folly's brink,
So rarely deigns the world to think.
Yet, ere I go, child of my heart—
One faithful offering I'll impart
To thee—thy parents' sole delight:
To me—an angel, pure as light.
Sent on this earth to cheer and bless,
Like sunbeam in a wilderness,
With fascination's form and face,
And all the charms that please and grace.
A guileless heart, a lovely mind,
A temper ardent, yet refined,
And in the early dawn of youth,
Taught to love honour, faith, and truth.
Ah! these—when all the transient joys
Of idle life, when all its toys
Shall fade like mist before the sun,
Yet, ere thy little day is done,
Shall give that calm, that true delight,
Which gilds the darkling hues of night,
The sunset of a well spent day,
A glorious immortality!

ON READING THE POEM OF "PARIS" BY THE REV GEORGE CROLY, A.M.

Author of "The Angel of the World," "Sebastian," &c.

By the trim taper, and the blazing hearth,
  (While loud without the blast of winter sung),
Now thrill'd with awe, and now relax'd with mirth,
  Paris, I've roam'd thy varied haunts among,
Loitering where Fashion's insect myriads spread

Their painted wings, and sport their little day;
Anon, by beckoning recollection led
   To the dark shadow of the stern ABBAYE,
Pale Fancy heard the petrifying shriek
Of midnight Murder from its turrets bleak,
And to her horrent eye came passing on
Phantoms of those dark times, elapsed and gone,
   When Rapine yell'd o'er his defenceless prey,
As unchain'd Anarchy her tocsin rung,
   And France! in dust and blood thy throne and altars lay!
Oh! thou, thus skill'd with absolute controul,
Where'er thou wilt to lead th' admiring soul,
Gifted alike with Fancy's train to sport,
And tread light measures in her elfin court;
Or pierce the height where Grandeur sits alone,
Girt by the tempest, on his mountain throne:
Whate'er the theme which wakes thy vocal shell,
Well-pleased I follow where its concords swell;
In regal halls, where pleasure wings the night
With pomp and music, revelry and light,
Or where, unwept by Love's deploring eyes,
In the lone Morgue, the self-doom'd victim lies—
Then, midst the twilight of yon Chapel dim,
To mark Religion's reverend Martyr, him
Who kneels entranced in agony of prayer,
His fellow victims torpid with despair,
Thrill'd by his piercing tones, his beaming eye
Glows, as he glows, nor longer dread to die!
Now, borne to Belgium's plain on bolder wings,
Where England's warriors fix'd the fate of Kings:
At once the Patriot and the Poet glows,
And full the mingling inspiration flows:—
Resume the lyre: not thine in myrtle bowers
To trifle light with Life's uncounted hours—
To crown thy toils, propitious Fame from far
Entwines her noblest wreath, illumes her loftiest star!

WRITTEN ON THE DEATH OF GENERAL SIR RALPH ABERCROMBIE

Mute Memory stands at Valour's awful shrine,
 In tears Britannia mourns her hero dead;
A world's regret, brave ABERCROMBIE's thine,
 For nature sorrow'd as thy spirit fled!
For, not the tear that matchless courage claims,
 To honest zeal, and soft compassion due,
Alone is thine—o'er thy adored remains

Each virtue weeps, for all once lived in you.
Yes, on thy deeds exulting I could dwell,
 To speak the merits of thy honour'd name;
But, ah! what need my humble muse to tell,
 When Rapture's self has echoed forth thy fame?
Yet, still thy name its energies shall deal,
 When wild storms gather round thy country's sun;
Her glowing youth shall grasp the gleamy steel,
 Rank'd round the glorious wreaths which thou hast won!

WRITTEN IN THE ALBUM OF I— H— P—, ESQ.

Dear P—, while Painters, Poets, Sages,
Inscribe this volume's votive pages
With partial friendship: why invite
The tribute of a luckless wight
Unknown—by wisdom or by wit
Indulged with no certificate?
Perchance, as in a diadem
Glittering with many a radiant gem,
Some mean metallic foil is placed
Judicious, by the hand of taste;
You seek, amidst the sons of fame,
To set an undistinguish'd name?
If so—that name is freely lent,
A pebble to your gems—T. GENT.

RETALIATION

Love, Cupid, Gallantry, whate'er
We call that elf, seen every where,
Half frolicsome, half ennuyeuse,
Had chanced a country walk to choose;
When sudden, sweet and bright as May,
Young Beauty tripp'd across his way.—
"Upon my word," exclaims the boy,
"A lucky hit! this pretty toy
To pass an hour, with vapours haunted,
Is quite the thing I wish'd and wanted;
I do not so far condescend
As serious mischief to intend,
But just to show my powers of pleasing
In flattery, badinage, and teasing;
But should she, for young girls, poor things!

Are tender as yon insect's wings—
Should she mistake me, and grow fond,
Why, I'll grow serious—and abscond."
First, not abruptly to confound her,
With glance and smile he hovers round her:
Next, like a Bond-street or Pall-mall beau,
Begins to press her gentle elbow;
Then plays at once, familiar walking,
His whole artillery of talking:—
Like a young fawn the blushing maid
Trips on, half pleased and half afraid—
And while she palpitates and listens,
Still fluttering where the sunbeam glistens,
He shows her all his pretty things,
His bow and quiver, dart, and wings;
Now, proud in power, he sees her eyes
Dilate with beautiful surprise;
But most, though fraught with perturbation.
His weapons claim her admiration,
And with an archness most bewitching
(Her naive simplicity enriching),
She wonders where a maid might buy than,
And begs to be allow'd to try them.
With secret scorn, but smiling bland,
He yields them to her curious hand,
When, instant, twang! the arrow flew,
So just her aim, it pierced him through,
Right through his heart, the luckless lad!
(A heart, to do him right, he had);
All prone he lies, in throbbing anguish,
Through many an hour to pine and languish,
And what made all his pangs more bitter,
Off flew the damsel in a titter.
Prudence, conceal'd behind a tree,
Cries out, "you've always laughed at me—
Henceforth you'll recollect, young sir!
'Tis not so safe to laugh at her."

LINES WRITTEN IN A COPY OF THE POEM ON PRINCESS CHARLOTTE

Presented to Mrs. D— T—.

Madam! when sorrowing o'er the virtuous dead,
The gentlest solace of the tears we shed,
Is, to surviving excellence to turn,
And honour there those merits that we mourn.

The Muse, whose hand fair Brunswick's ashes strew
With votive flowers, would weave a wreath for You;
But living worth forbids th' applausive lay.
Therefore, repressing all respect, would say,
She proffers silently her simple strain;
If you approve—she has not toil'd in vain!

SONNET

When the rough storm roars round the peasant's cot,
  And bursting thunders roll their awful din;
While shrieks the frighted night-bird o'er the spot,
  Oh! what serenity remains within!
For there contentment, health, and peace, abide,
  And pillow'd age, with calm eye fix'd above;
Labour's bold son, his blithe and blooming bride,
  And lisping innocence, and filial love.
To such a scene let proud Ambition turn,
  Whose aching breast conceals its secret woe;
Then shall his fireful spirit melt, and mourn
  The mild enjoyments it can never know;
Then shall he feel the littleness of state,
And sigh that fortune e'er had made him great.

TO ROBERT SOUTHEY, ESQ.

ON READING HIS "REMAINS OF HENRY KIRKE WHITE"

Southey! high placed on the contested throne
Of modern verse, a Muse, herself unknown,
Sues that her tears may consecrate the strains
Pour'd o'er the urn enrich'd with WHITE'S Remains!
While touch'd to transport, Taste's responding tone
Makes the rapt poet's ecstasies thine own;
Ah! think that he, whose hand supremely skill'd,
The heart's fine chords with deep vibration thrill'd,
In stagnant silence and petrific gloom,
Unconscious sleeps, the tenant of the tomb!
Extinct that spirit, whose strong-bidding drew
From Fancy's confines Wonder's wild-eyed crew,
Which bade Despair's terrific phantoms pass
Like Macbeth's monarchs in the mystic glass.
Before the youthful bard's impassion'd eye,
Like him, led on, to triumph and to die;

Like him, by mighty magic compass'd round,
And seeking sceptres on enchanted ground.
Such spells invest, such blear illusion waits
The trav'ller bound for Fame's receding gates,
Delusive splendours gild the proud abode,
But lurking demons haunt th' alluring road;
There gaunt-eyed Want asserts her iron reign,
There, as in vengeance of the world's disdain,
This half-flesh'd hag midst Wit's bright blossoms stalks,
And, breathing winter, withers where she walks;
Though there, long outlaw'd, desp'rate with disgrace,
Invidious Dulness wields the critic mace,
And sworn in hate, exerts his ruffian might
Where'er young genius meditates his flight.
Erewhile, when WHITE, by this fell fiend oppress'd,
Felt Hope's fine fervours languish in his breast,
When shrunk with scorn, and trembling to aspire,
He dropp'd desponding his insulted lyre.
Alert in zeal, with art benign endued,
SOUTHEY! thy hand his blasted strength renew'd,
And lured him on, his labours scarce begun,
To win those laurels which thyself had won.
In vain! though vivified with pristine force,
O'er learning's realms he shot with meteor course;
To worth relentless, Fate's despotic frown
Scowl'd in the bright perspective of renown:
Timeless he falls, in Death's pale triumph led.
And his first laurels shade his grassy bed.
So sinks the Muse's offspring, doom'd to try,
Like a caged eagle panting tow'rds the sky,
A foil'd ascent, while adverse fortune flings
Her strong link'd meshes o'er his flutt'ring wings,
Sinks, while exalted Ignorance supine,
Unheeded slumbers like the pamper'd swine;
Obsequious slaves in his voluptuous bowers
Young pleasures warble, while the dancing Hours
In sickly sweetness languishingly move,
Like new-waked virgins flush'd with dreams of love—
Him, when by Death's dark angel swept away
From sloth's embrace, in premature decay,
Surviving friends, donation'd into grief,
Shall mourn with anguish audible and brief,
And pander-bards ring round in goodly chime
His liberal heart, high wit, and soul sublime;
But Flattery's frauds impartial Time disowns,
Funereal pomp, and adulative tones;
Slow where she moves through monumental aisles,
With stern contempt insulted Reason smiles,

While Falsehood, shrined above th' emblazon'd palls,
Shames sanctity from consecrated walls:
She seeks, with pensive step and saintly eyes,
Some lonely grave, where rude the grass-tufts rise;
Nor sculptured angels tell, nor chisell'd lines,
There slumbers CHATTERTON—here WHITE reclines!
But nobler triumphs WHITE'S probation claims
Than ever blazon'd Wit's recorded names;
For Virtue's sons, to bliss immortal born,
Tower to their native heaven, and view with scorn
The vain distinction of the trophied sod,
'Tis theirs to gain distinction with their God!

THE STATE SECRET

AN IMPROMPTU

"Murder will out:"—and so will truth sometimes;
For once I'll prove it in a dozen lines.—
At one of those parties where Julia's sweet face
Added interest to beauty, and archness to grace,
Where many fine folks met; and one very great,
Proud and stupid, an embryo minister sate;
Like a damper he came to put good humour out,
And it chanced that, as Julia's pet-bird flew about.
It presumptuously 'lit on this mighty man's head;
When her lore-laughing sister, sweet Eleanor, said,
"Naughty bird! I must cage you for being so rude,
On Lord———head, oh! how dare you intrude?"
"Let it rest," replied Julia, with an exquisite grace,
"Don't frighten it off—for it likes a soft place!"

THE MORNING CALL

TO THE HONOURABLE LADY —

Written and left on her Table during her absence—Bathing.

I dare not look at those dear eyes,
  The sun was never half so bright,
There surely more of rapture lies
  Than ever bless'd a mortal's sight.
In thy sweet face I see impress'd
  Ten thousand thousand charms divine,

The sunbeams of thy guileless breast
  Like Heaven's eternal mercies shine!
Angel of love! life's endless joy,
  Our hope at morn, our evening prayer;
The bliss above would have alloy,
  Unless dear — thou wert there!
Oh! Woman—what a charm hast thou
  Our rebel nature thus to tame:
We ever must adore and bow.
  While virtue guards thy holy fane!
Werthing.

SONNET

ON THE DEATH OF TOUSSAINT L'OUVERTURE

His weary warfare done, his woes forgot,
  Freedom! thy son, oppress'd so long, is free:
He seeks the realms where tyranny is not,
  And those shall hail him who have died for thee!
Immortal TELL! receive a soul like thine,
  Who scorn'd obedience to usurp'd command:
Who rose a giant from a sphere indign,
  To tear the rod from proud oppression's hand.
Alas! no victor-wreaths enzon'd his brow,
  But freedom long his hapless fate shall mourn;
Her holy tears shall nurse the laurel-bough,
  Whose green leaves grace his consecrated urn.
Nursed by these tears, that bough shall rise sublime,
  And bloom triumphant 'mid the wrecks of time!

ON THE RUPTURE OF THE THAMES' TUNNEL, WRITTEN 2nd JULY, 1827

Every poor Quidnunc now condemns
The Tunnel underneath Old Thames,
And swears, his science all forgetting,
Friend Brunel's judgment wanted whetting;
'Tis thus great characters are dish'd,
When they get wetter than was wish'd,—
Brunel to Gravesend meant to go
Under the water, wags say so,
And under that same water put
His hopes to find a shorter cut;
But when we leave the light of day.

Water hath many a devious way,
Which, like a naughty woman, leads
The best of men to strange misdeeds:
Had nearly, 'twas a toss-up whether,
Gone to his grave and end together.
How the performance went amiss
The classical account is this—
The Naiads, Thames' stream that swim in,
Being curious, just like mortal women,
Dear souls! 'tis said, midst all their cares,
They love to peep at man's affairs,
And wondering at the workmen's hammers,
The noise of axes, engines, rammers,
Thought 'twould be well, nor meant the fun ill,
To make an opening through the Tunnel,
Just to see how the work went on,
And then, down dash'd they, every one;
When these same belles began to dire,
'Twas well the workmen 'scaped alive:
Brunel, indeed, who knew full well
The nature of a diving bell,
Remain'd some time, nor made wry faces,
Within their aqueous embraces;
Nay, fierce and ungallant, adventured
To oust them by the breach they entered.
Vain man! 'twas well that he could swim,
Or, certes, they had ousted him.
Speed on great projects! though we rate 'em
Rash, for alluvial pomatum,
And under that a sandy stratum,
Will offer at a little distance
An insurmountable resistance.
How strange! to find the labour done
Just as the sand begins to run;
In general human projects drop,
Just when our sand begins to stop!

ANACREONTIC

"THE WISEST MEN ARE FOOLS IN WINE"

The wisest men are fools in wine,
  Experience makes us think:
Its magic spells are so divine,
  We reason—yet we drink!
How short's the longest life of man,

How soon its brightest laurels fade—
Then, as our life is but a span,
   Let all its hours be joyous made.
Wine o'er the ardent restless mind
   Entwines its poppy chain;
A solace, then, the wretched find.
   In fictions of the brain.
Oh! as the charmed glass we sip,
We conquer care and pain:
It woos like woman's dewy lip,
To kiss—and come again!

LINES WRITTEN IN HORNSEY WOOD

Oh! ye, who pine, in London smoke immured,
With spirits wearied, and with pains uncured,
With all the catalogue of city evils,
Colds, asthmas, rheumatism, coughs, blue devils!
Who bid each bold empiric roll in wealth,
Who drains your fortunes while he saps your health:
So well ye love your dirty streets and lanes,
Ye court your ailments and embrace your pains.
And scarce ye know, so little have ye seen,
If corn be yellow, or if grass be green;
Why leave ye not your smoke-obstructed holes,
With wholesome air to cheer your sickly souls?
In scenes where Health's bright goddess wakes the breeze,
Floats on the stream, and fans the whisp'ring trees:
Soon would the brighten'd eye her influence speak,
And her full roses flush the faded cheek.
Then, where romantic Hornsey courts the eye
With all the charms of sylvan scenery,
Let the pale sons of Diligence repair,
And pause, like me, from sedentary care;
Here the rich landscape spreads profusely wide,
And here embowering shades the prospect hide:
Each mazy walk in wild meanders moves,
And infant oaks, luxuriant, grace the groves:
Oaks, that by time matured, removed afar,
Shall ride triumphant, 'midst the wat'ry war;
Shall blast the bulwarks of Britannia's foes,
And claim her empire, wide as ocean flows!
O'er all the scene, mellifluous and bland,
The blissful powers of harmony expand;
Soft sigh the zephyrs 'mid the still retreats,
And steal from Flora's lips ambrosial sweets;

Their notes of love the feather'd songsters sing,
And Cupid peeps behind the vest of Spring.
Ye swains! who ne'er obtain'd with all your sighs
One tender look from Chloe's sparkling eyes,
In shades like these her cruelty assail,
Here, whisper soft your amatory tale;
The scene to sympathy the maid shall move,
And smiles propitious crown your slighted love.
While the fresh air with fragrance summer fills,
And lifts her voice, heard jocund o'er the hills,
All jubilant the waving woods display
Her gorgeous gifts, magnificently gay!
The wond'ring eye beholds these waving woods
Reflected bright in artificial floods,
And still, the tufts of clust'ring shrubs between,
Like passing sprites, the nymphs and swains are seen;
Till fancy triumphs in th'exulting breast,
And Care shrinks back, astonish'd! dispossess'd!
For all breathes rapture, all enchantment seems,
Like fairy visions, and poetic dreams!
Though on such scenes the fancy loves to dwell,
The stomach oft a different tale will tell;
Then, leave the wood, and seek the shelt'ring roof,
And put the pantry's vital strength to proof;
The aërial banquets of the tuneful nine
May suit some appetites, but faith! not mine;
For my coarse palate coarser food must please,
Substantial beef, pies, puddings, ducks, and peas;
Such food the fangs of keen disease defies,
And such rare feeding Hornsey-house supplies:
Nor these alone the joys that court us here,
Wine! generous wine! that drowns corroding care,
Asserts its empire in the glittering bowl,
And pours Promethean vigour o'er the soul.
Here, too, that bluff John Bull, whose blood boils high
At such base wares of foreign luxury;
Who scorns to revel in imported cheer,
Who prides in perry, and exults in beer:
On these his surly virtue shall regale,
With quickening cyder, and with fattening ale.
Nor think, ye Fair! our Hornsey has denied
The elegant repasts where you preside:
Here, may the heart rejoice, expanding free
In all the social luxury of Tea!
Whose essence pure inspires such charming chat,
With nods, and winks, and whispers, and all that;
Here, then, while 'wrapt inspired, like Horace old,
We chant convivial hymns to Bacchus bold;

Or heave the incense of unconscious sighs,
To catch the grace that beams from beauty's eyes;
Or, in the winding wilds, sequester'd deep,
Th' unwilling Muse invoking, fall asleep;
Or cursing her, and her ungranted smiles,
Chase butterflies along the echoing aisles:
Howe'er employ'd, here be the town forgot,
Where fogs, and smoke, and jostling crowds, are not.

TO MARY

WRITTEN AT MIDNIGHT

Oh! is there not in infant smiles
  A witching power, a cheering ray,
A charm, that every care beguiles,
  And bids the weary soul be gay?
There surely is—for thou hast been,
  Child of my heart, my peaceful dove,
Gladdening life's sad and chequer'd scene,
  An emblem of the peace above.
Now all is calm, and dark, and still,
  And bright the beam the moonlight throws
On ocean wave, and gentle rill,
  And on thy slumbering cheek of rose.
And may no care disturb that breast,
  Nor sorrow dim that brow serene;
And may thy latest years be bless'd
  As thy sweet infancy has been.

BLACK EYES AND BLUE

FROM THE ITALIAN

Blue eyes and jet
  Fell out one morn,
Azure cried in a pet,
  "Away, dark scorn!—
"We are brilliant and blue
  "As the waves of the sea—
"And as cold and untrue
  "And as changeable ye.
"We are born of the sky,
  "Of a summer night,

"When the first stars lie
  "In a bed of blue light;
"From the cloudy zone
  "Round the setting sun,
"Like an angel's throne,
  "Are our glories won."
"Pretty ladies, hold,"
  Cupid said to the eyes—
For beauties that scold
  "Are seldom wise;
"'Tis not colour I seek
  "Love's fires to impart—
"Give me eyes that can speak
  "From the depths of the heart."

EPIGRAM

AURI SACRA FAMES

I knew a being once, his peaked head
With a few lank and greasy hairs was spread;
His visage blue, in length was like your own
Seen in the convex of a table-spoon.
His mouth, or rather gash athwart his face,
To stop at either ear had just the grace,
A hideous rift: his teeth were all canine,
And just like Death's (in Milton) was his grin.
One shilling, and one fourteen-penny leg,
(This shorter was than that, and not so big),
He had; and they, when meeting at his knees,
An angle formed of ninety-eight degrees.
Nature, in scheming how his back to vary,
A hint had taken from the dromedary:
His eyes an inward, screwing vision threw,
Striving each other through his nose to view.
His intellect was just one ray above
The idiot Cymon's ere he fell in love.
At school they Taraxippus[1] called the wight;
The Misses, when they met him, shriek'd with fright.
But, spite of all that Nature had denied,
When sudden Fortune made the cub her pride,
And gave him twenty thousand pounds a-year,
Then, from the pretty Misses you might hear,
"His face was not the finest, and, indeed,
He was a little, they must own, in-kneed;
His shoulders, certainly, were rather high,

But, then, he had a most expressive eye;
Nor were their hearts by outward charms inclined:
Give them the higher beauties of the mind!"

[Footnote 1: Greek: Taraxippus, a Grecian Deity; the god of the Hippodrome, literally, in English, horse-frightener.]

TO FAITH

Hail! holy FAITH, on life's wide ocean toss'd,
  I see thee sit calm in thy beaten bark;
  As NOAH sat, throned in his high-borne ark,
Secure and fearless while a world was lost!
In vain contending storms thy head enzone,
  Thy bosom shrinks not from the bolt that falls:
  The dreadful shaft plays harmless, nor appals
Thy stedfast eye, fix'd on Jehovah's throne!
E'en though thou saw'st the mighty fabric nod,
  Of system'd worlds, thou hear'st a sacred charm,
  Graved on thy heart, to shelter thee from harm.
And thus it speaks:—"Thou art my trust, O GOD!
And thou canst bid the jarring-powers be still,
Each ponderous orb, subservient to thy will!"

ON A SPIRITED PORTRAIT IN MY ALBUM

Of a favorite Deer-hound, belonging to SIR WALTER SCOTT, by my friend, EDWIN LANDSEER, Esq.

Who in this sketchey wonder does not trace
The fire, the spirit, and the living grace,
That mark the hand of genius and of taste?
Who does not recognize in such a head
Truth, vigilance, fidelity, inbred,
Sagacity that's human, and a waste
Of those high qualities, and virtues rare,
Which poor humanity has not to spare?
Then, faithful Hound! thy happy lot is cast
In pleasant places—and thy life has pass'd
In the dear service of a Master—whom
The world's concurrent voice has yielded now
The meed of highest praise—and on whose brow
Th' imperishable wreath of fame shall bloom;

Nor is this fate less happy than the rest,
That he should paint thee, who can paint thee best!

SONNET

TO HOPE

How droops the wretch whom adverse fates pursue,
  While sad experience, from his aching sight
  Sweeps the fair prospects of unproved delight,
Which flattering friends and flattering fancies drew.
When want assails his solitary shed,
  When dire distraction's horrent eye-ball glares,
  Seen 'midst the myriad of tumultuous cares,
That shower their shafts on his devoted head.
Then, ere despair usurp his vanquish'd heart,
  Is there a power, whose influence benign
  Can bid his head in pillow'd peace recline,
And from his breast withdraw the barbed dart?
There is—sweet Hope! misfortune rests on thee—
Unswerving anchor of humanity!

LINES WRITTEN ON THE SIXTH OF SEPTEMBER

Ill-fated hour! oft as thy annual reign
Leads on th' autumnal tide, my pinion'd joys
Fade with the glories of the fading year;
"Remembrance wakes, with all her busy train,"
And bids affection heave the heart-drawn sigh
O'er the cold tomb, rich with the spoils of death,
And wet with many a tributary tear!
Eight times has each successive season sway'd
The fruitful sceptre of our milder clime
Since my loved——died! but why, ah! why
Should melancholy cloud my early years?
Religion spurns earth's visionary scene,
Philosophy revolts at misery's chain:
Just Heaven recall'd its own; the pilgrim call'd
From human woes: from sorrow's rankling worm—
Shall frailty then prevail?
        Oh! be it mine
To curb the sigh which bursts o'er Heaven's decree;
To tread the path of rectitude—that when
Life's dying ray shall glimmer in the frame,

That latest breath I may in peace resign,
"Firm in the faith of seeing thee and God."

SONNET

TO CHARITY

O! best-beloved of Heaven, on earth bestow'd,
  To raise the pilgrim sunk with ghastly fears,
  To cool his burning wounds, to wipe his tears,
And strew with amaranths his thorny road.
Alas! how long has Superstition hurl'd
  Thine altars down, thine attributes reviled,
  The hearts of men with witchcrafts foul beguiled.
And spread his empire o'er the vassal world?
But truth returns! she spreads resistless day;
  And mark, the monster's cloud-wrapt fabric falls—
  He shrinks—he trembles 'mid his inmost halls,
And all his damn'd illusions melt away!
The charm dissolved—immortal, fair, and free,
Thy holy fanes shall rise, celestial Charity!

HYMN

Sung by the Children of the City of London School of Instruction and Industry

CHORUS
Sacred, and heart-deep be the sound
  Which speaks the Great Redeemer's praise,
His mercies every where abound,
  Let all their grateful voices raise.

BOYS
The friendless child, to manhood grown,
  Will ne'er forget your parent care;
You've made each youthful heart your own,
  Oh! then accept our humble prayer.

GIRLS
For ever be that bounty praised,
  Which every comfort doth impart;
In tears of joy the song is raised
  From minstrels of the glowing heart.

CHORUS

Glory to Thee, all-bounteous Power!
  In notes of thankfulness be given;
Sure solace in affliction's hour!
  Our hope on Earth, our bliss in Heaven.
        Hallelujah! Amen.

REFLECTIONS OF A POET, ON GOING TO A GREAT DINNER

Great epoch in the history of bards!
  Important day to those who woo the nine;
Better than fame are visitation-cards,
  And heaven on earth at a great house to dine.
O cruel memory! do not conjure up
  The ghost of Sally Dab, the famous cook;
Who gave me solid food, the cheering cup,
  And on her virtues begg'd I'd write a book.
For her dear sake I braved the letter'd fates,
  And all her loose thoughts in one volume cramm'd;
"The Accomplish'd Cook, in verse, with twenty plates:"
  Which (O! ungrateful deed!) the critics d——d.
D—n them, I say, the tasteless envious elves;
  Malicious fancy makes them so expert,
They write 'bout dinners, who ne'er dine themselves,
  And boast of linen, who ne'er had a shirt.
Rest, goddess, from all broils! I bless thy name,
  Dear kitchen-nymph, as ever eyes did glut on!
I'd give thee all I have, my slice of fame,
  If thou, fat shade! could'st give one slice of mutton.
Yet hold—ten minutes more, and I am bless'd;
  Fly quick, ye seconds; quick, ye moments, fly:
Soon shall I put my hunger to the test,
  And all the host of miseries defy.
Thrice is he arm'd, who hath his dinner first,
  For well-fed valour always fights the best;
And though he may of over-eating burst,
  His life is happy, and his death is just.
To-day I dine—not on my usual fare;
  Not near the sacred mount with skinny nine;
Not in the park upon a dish of air:
  But on true eatables, and rosy wine.
Delightful task! to cram the hungry maw,
  To teach the empty stomach how to fill,
To pour red port adown the parched craw;
  Without that dread dessert—to pay the bill.
I'm off—methinks I smell the long-lost savour;

Hail, platter-sound! to poet music sweet:
Now grant me, Jove, if not too great a favour,
  Once in my life as much as I can eat!

SUNDAY

Come, thou blessed day of rest!
Soother of the tortured breast,
Wearied souls release from toil,
Life's eternal sad turmoil;
How I love thy tuneful bells
Which a welcome story tells!
Bids the wanderer rest and pray
On this peaceful holy-day.
All creation seems to pause—
Man, uncatechized by laws,
Looks to God with grateful eyes,
In such blessed sympathies,
All his rebel nature dies!
See the monster crime hath made,
Resting from his restless trade,
Unfit to live, afraid to die,
Hear his deep unconscious sigh,
See his former horrid mien,
Changed to the bright, serene,
View him on his BIBLE rest,
Care no longer gnaws his breast;
Heaven, in mercy, let him live,
Religion, such the peace you give!

A NIGHT-STORM

Let this rough fragment lend its mossy seat;
Let Contemplation hail this lone retreat:
Come, meek-eyed goddess, through the midnight gloom,
Born of the silent awe which robes the tomb!
This gothic front, this antiquated pile,
The bleak wind howling through each mazy aisle;
Its high gray towers, faint peeping through the shade,
Shall hail thy presence, consecrated maid!
Whether beneath some vaulted abbey's dome,
Where ev'ry footstep sounds in every tomb;
Where Superstition, from the marble stone,
Gives every sound, a pilgrim-spirit's groan:

Pensive thou readest by the moon's full glare
The sculptured children of Affection's tear;
Or in the church-yard lone thou sitt'st to weep
O'er some sad wreck, beneath the tufty heap—
Perchance some victim to Seduction's spell,
Who yielded, wept, and then neglected fell!
But hither come, on yon swoln arch to gaze,
And view the vivid flash eruptive blare;
Light those high walls with transitory gleam,
Illume the air, and sparkle in the stream.
Ah! look, where yonder tempest-shaken cloud,
Awful and black as the chaosian shroud,
Breaks, like the waves which lash the sandy shore,
And speaks its mission in a feeble row.
Thus Meditation hears: "Aspiring height!
Of old, the splendid mansions of the great;
Thy fate (tremendous) lours upon the blast,
And waits to write on thy remains:—'tis past!
Oft have the genii of the hoary blade
Around thy walls their hell-born demons led;
Yet hast thou triumph'd o'er each monster's car,
And braved the ills of pestilential war:
Oft hast thou seen the circling seasons roll
In fond succession round thy native pole;
Defied the hoary matron of the ring,
And seen her sicken in the lap of Spring.
But, ah! no more thy time-clad head shall rise
To dare the tempest, while it shakes the skies;
Nor one small wreck invade the fair concave,
Nor shout above its crumbling basis, Save!
When rising zephyr from thy ruin brings
A world of atoms on its fairy wings."
Din horrible! as though the rebel train
Had sprung from chaos, fought, and fall'n again,
Raves the high bolt: how yon old structure fell;
How every cranny trembled with the yell
Of frighted owls, whose secret haunts forlorn
Were from their kindred vaults and windings torn;
Of bold Antiquity's rough pencil born.
Thrice Fancy leads the dismal echo round,
And paints the spectre gliding o'er the ground.
From ev'ry turret, ev'ry vanquish'd tower,
In heaps confused the broken fragments pour;
And, as they plunge toward the pebbly grave,
Like wizard wand, draw circles in the wave.
Meand'ring stream! thy liquid jaws extend,
Anoint with Lethe now thy fallen friend.
Again the heralds of the thunder fly,

In forky squadrons, from the trembling sky!
Again the thunder its harsh menace swells,
And light-wing'd echoes hail the humbled cells!
Weep, weep, ye clouds! with heav'n-bespangled tears;
And, ah! if pity rules your sacred spheres,
Invoke the thunder to withstay its rage,
Disarm its fury, and its wrath assuage.
But now, Aurora, from the Ocean's verge,
Trims her gray lamp, to light the mournful dirge.
She comes, to light the ruinated heap:
But lights, to wake the pensive soul to weep!

ON THE DEATH OF NELSON

Swift through the land while Fame transported flies,
And shouts triumphant shake th' illumined skies;
Britannia, bending o'er her dauntless prows,
With laurels thickening round her blazon'd brows,
In joy dejected, sees her triumph cross'd,
Exults in Victory won, but mourns the Victor lost.
Immortal NELSON! still with fond amaze
Thy glorious deed each British eye surveys,
Beholds thee still, on conquer'd floods afar:
Fate's flaming shaft! the thunderbolt of war!
Hurl'd from thy hands, Britannia's vengeance roars,
And bloody billows stain the hostile shores:
Thy sacred ire Confed'rate Kingdoms braves,
And 'whelms their Navies in Sepulchral waves!
—Graced with each attribute which Heaven supplies
To Godlike Chiefs: humane, intrepid, wise:
His Nation's Bulwark, and all Nature's pride,
The Hero lived, and as he lived—he died:
Transcendant destiny! how bless'd the brave,
Whose fall his Country's tears attend, shower'd on his trophied grave!

THE BLUE-EYED MAID

Sweet are the hours when roseate spring
  With health and joy salutes the day.
When zephyr, borne on wanton wing,
  Soft whispering, wakes the blushing May.
Sweet are the hours, yet not so sweet
As when my blue-eyed Maid I meet,
And hear her soul-entrancing tale,

Sequester'd in the shadowy vale.
The mellow horn's long-echoing notes
  Startle the morn, commingling strong;
At eve, the harp's wild music floats.
  And ravish'd Silence drinks the song.
Yet sweeter is the song of love,
When EMMA'S voice enchants the grove,
While listening sylphs repeat the tale,
Sequester'd in the silent vale.

TAKING ORDERS

A TALE, FOUNDED ON FACT

A parson once—and poorer he
Than ever parson ought to be;
Yet not so proud as some from College,
Who fancy they alone have knowledge;
Who only learn to dress and drink,
And, strange to say, still seem to think
That no real talent's to be found
Except within their classic ground;
Yet prove that Cam's nor Oxon's plains
Can't furnish empty skulls with brains.
But for my tale—Our churchman came,
And, in religion's honour'd name,
Sought Cam's delightful classic borders,
To be prefer'd to Holy Orders.
Chance led him to the Trav'llers' Inn,
Where living's cheap, and often whim
Enlivens many a weary soul,
And helps, in the o'erflowing bowl,
In spite of fogs, and threatening weather,
To drown both grief and gloom together:—
(Oh, Wit! thou'rt like a little blue,
Soft cloud, in summer breaking through
A frowning one, and lighting it
Till darkness fadeth bit by bit;
And Whim to thee is near allied,
And follows closely at thy side;
So oft, oh, Wit! I'm told that she
By some folks is mista'en for thee;
Yet I may say unto my eyes,
Just whereabouts the difference lies;
One's diamond quite, and, to my taste,
The other is but Dovey's Paste.)—

He there a ready welcome found
From one who travell'd England round:
"Sir, your obedient—quite alone?
I'm truly happy you are come:
Pray, sir, be seated;—business dull;—
Or else this room had now been full;
Orders and cash are strangers here,
And every thing looks dev'lish queer;
Bad times these, sir, sad lack of wealth;
Must hope for better;—Sir, your health!"
Then added, with inquiring face,
"Come to take Orders in this place?"
"Yes, sir, I am," replied the priest:
"With that intent I came at least."
"Ha! ha! I knew it very well;
We business-men can others tell:
Often before I've seen your face,
Though memory can't recal the place—
Ah! now I have it; head of mine!
You travel in the button line?"
"Begging your pardon, sir, I fear
Some error has arisen here;
You have mista'en my trade divine,
But, sir, the worldly loss is mine—
I travel in a much worse line."

THE GIPSY'S HOME

A GLEE

Sung by Messrs. PYNE, NELSON, Miss WITHAM, and Master LONGHURST.—Composed by Mr. ROOKE.

We, who the wide world make our home;
  The barren heath our cheerful bed;
Careless o'er mount and moor we roam,
  And never tears of sorrow shed.
        But merrily, O! Merrily, O!
        Through this world of care we go.
Love, that a palace left in tears,
  Flew to our houseless feast of mirth:
For here, unfetter'd, beauty cheers,
  The heaven alone that's found on earth!
        Then merrily, O! Merrily, O!
        Through this world of care we go.

SONNET

THE BEGGAR

Of late I saw him on his staff reclined,
  Bow'd down beneath a weary weight of woes,
Without a roof to shelter from the wind
  His head, all hoar with many a winter's snows.
All trembling he approach'd, he strove to speak;
  The voice of misery scarce my ear assail'd;
A flood of sorrow swept his furrow'd cheek,
  Remembrance check'd him, and his utt'rance fail'd.
For he had known full many a better day;
  And when the poor man at his threshold bent,
He drove him not with aching heart away,
  But freely shared what Providence had sent.
How hard for him, the stranger's boon to crave,
And live to want the mite his bounty gave!

TO —.

Come, JENNY, let me sip the dew
  That on those coral lips doth play,
One kiss would every care subdue,
  And bid my weary soul be gay.
For surely thou wert form'd by love
  To bless the suff'rer's parting sigh;
In pity then my griefs remove,
  And on that bosom let me die!

SONG

THE RECAL OF THE HERO

When Discord blew her fell alarm
  On Gallia's blood-stain'd ground,
When Usurpation's giant arm
  Enslaved the nations round:
The thunders of avenging Heaven
To NELSON'S chosen hand were given!
By NELSON'S chosen hand were hurl'd,
To rescue the devoted world!
The tyrant power, his vengeance dread

To Egypt's shores pursued;
At Trafalgar its hydra-head
  For ever sunk subdued.
The freedom of mankind was won!
The hero's glorious task was done!
When Heaven, Oppression's ensigns furl'd,
Recall'd him from the rescued world.

TO ELIZA

WRITTEN IN HER ALBUM

I dare not spoil this spotless page
  With any feeble verse of mine;
The Poet's fire has lost its rage,
  Around his lyre no myrtles twine.
The voice of fame cannot recal
  Those fairy days of past delight,
When pleasure seem'd to welcome all,
  And morning hail'd a welcome night.
E'en love has lost its soothing power,
  Its spells no more can chain my soul;
I must not venture in the bower,
  Where Wit and Verse and Wine controul.
And yet, I fear, in thoughtless mirth
  I once did say, Eliza, dear!
That I would tell the world thy worth,
  And write the living record here.
Come Love, and Truth, and Friendship, come,
  Enwreath'd in Virtue's snowy arms,
With magic rhymes the page illume,
  And fancy sketch her varied charms—
Which o'er the cares of home has thrown
  A thousand blessings, deep engraved,
For every heart she makes her own,
  And every friend is free-enslaved.
No Inspiration o'er my pen
  Glows with the lightning's vivid spell;
My soul is sad—forgive me then,
  My heart's too full the tale to tell!
Yet, if the humblest poet's theme
  Be welcome in Eliza's name;
Then, angel, give the cheering gleam,
  For thy approving smile is fame!

ELEGY

On THE DEATH OF

ABRAHAM GOLDSMID, ESQ.

When stern Misfortune, monitress severe!
  Dissolves Prosperity's enchanting dreams,
And, chased from Man's probationary sphere,
  Fair Hope withdraws her vivifying beams.
If then, untaught to bend at Heaven's high will,
  The desp'rate mortal dares the dread unknown,
To future fate appeals from present ill,
  And stands, uncall'd, before th' Eternal throne!
Shall justice there immutably decide?
  Dread thought! which Reason trembles to explore,
She feels, be mercy granted or denied,
  'Tis her's in dumb submission to adore.
Yet, could the self-doom'd victim be forgiven
  His final error, for his merits past;
Could virtuous life, propitiating Heaven
  With former deeds, extenuate the last:
Then GOLDSMID! Mercy, to thy humble shrine,
  Angel of heaven beloved, should wing her flight,
Should in her bosom bid thy head recline,
  And waft thee onward to the realms of light.
And, oh! could human intercession plead,
  Breathed ardent to'ards that undiscover'd shore,
What hearts unnumber'd for thy fate that bleed,
  Would warm oblations for thy pardon pour.
Misfortune's various tribes thy worth should tell,
  Whose acts to no peculiar sect confined;
Impartial, with expansive bounty fell,
  Like heaven's refreshing dews on all mankind.
Where stern Disease his rankling arrows sped,
  While Want, with hard inexorable band,
Strew'd keener thorns on Pain's afflictive bed,
  And urged the flight of life's diminish'd sand.
By hostile stars oppress'd, where Talent toil'd,
  Encountering fate with perseverance vain;
The Merchant's hopes, when War's dire arm despoil'd,
  Or tempests 'whelm'd in the remorseless main.
GOLDSMID! thy hand benign assuagement spread,
  Sustain'd pale sickness, drooping o'er the tomb;
Raised modest Merit from his lowly shed,
  And gave Misfortune's blasted hopes to bloom.
Yet wealth, too oft perverted from its end,

Suspends the noblest functions of the soul;
  Where, chill'd as Apathy's cold frosts, extends,
  Compassion's sacred stream forgets to roll.
And oft, where seeming Pity moves the mind,
  From self's mean source the liberal current flows;
While Ostentation, insolently kind,
  Wounds while he soothes, insults while he bestows.
But thy free bounty, undebased by pride,
  Prompt to anticipate the meek request,
Unask'd the wants of modest Worth supplied,
  And spared the pang that shook the suppliant's breast.
Yet say! on Fortune's orb, which o'er thy head
  Blazed forth erewhile pre-eminently bright,
When dark Adversity her eclipse spread,
  And veil'd its splendours in petrific night!
Did those, thy benefits had placed on high,
  Who revell'd still in wealth's meridian ray;
Did those impatient to thy succour fly,
  Anxious the debt of gratitude to pay?
Or, thy fall'n fortunes coldly whispering round,
  Scowl'd they aloof in that disastrous hour?
On keen Misfortune's agonizing wound
  Did foul Ingratitude her poisons pour?
If thy distress such aggravation knew,
  Thy first reverse could such perdition wait;
Well might Despair thy generous heart subdue,
  And Desperation close the scene of fate.
Yet while Distraction urged her purpose dire,
  Rose not, at Nature's interposed command,
The sacred claims of Brother, Husband, Sire,
  To win the weapon from thy lifted hand?
Ah, yes! and ere that agony was o'er,
  Ere yet thy soul its last resolve embraced,
What pangs could equal those thy breast that tore,
  Thy breast with Nature's tenderest feelings graced?
Those only which, at thy accomplish'd fate,
  That home display'd, thy smiles were wont to bless;
That dreadful scene what language can relate,
  What words describe that exquisite distress.
The Muse recedes—in Grief's domestic scene
  Th' intrusive gaze prophanes the tears that flow:
Drop, Pity! there thy hallowed veil between;
  Guard, Silence! there the sacredness of woe.
Nor let the sectarist, whose faith austere
  Pretends alone to point th' eternal road;
Proud of his creed, pronounce with voice severe,
  All else excluded from the blest abode.
If error thine, not GOLDSMID! thine the fault,

Since first thy infant years instruction drew;
From youth's gradations up to manhood taught
  That faith to reverence which thy fathers knew.
In Retribution's last tremendous hour,
  When its pale captives, long in dust declined,
The grave shall yield, and time shall death devour,
  When He who saved, shall come to judge mankind.
While Christian-infidels shall tremble round,
  Who call'd HIM Master! whom their acts denied:
Imputed faith may in thy deeds be found,
  And thy eternal doom those deeds decide.

SONNET

ON THE DEATH OF MRS CHARLOTTE SMITH

Sweet songstress! whom the melancholy Muse
  With more than fondness loved, for thee she strung
  The lyre, on which herself enraptured hung,
And bade thee through the world its sweets diffuse.
Oft hath my childhood's tributary tear
  Paid homage to the sad harmonious strain,
  That told, alas! too true, the grief and pain
Which thy afflicted mind was doom'd to bear.
  Rest, sainted spirit! from a life of woe,
  And though no friendly hand on thee bestow
The stately marble, or emblazon'd name,
  To tell a thoughtless world who sleeps below:
  Yet o'er thy narrow bed a wreath shall blow.
Deriving vigour from the breath of fame!

MISTER PUNCH

A HASTY SKETCH

Who stops the Minister of State,
When hurrying to the Lords' debate?
Who, spite of gravity beguiles,
The solemn Bishop of his smiles?
See from the window, "burly big,"
The Judge pops out his awful wig,
Yet, seems to love a bit of gig!—While
both the Sheriffs and the Mayor
Forget the "Address"—and stop to stare—And

who detains the Husband true,
Running to Doctor Doode-Doo,
To save his Wife "in greatest danger;"
While e'en the Doctor keeps the stranger
Another hour from life and light,
To gape at the bewitching sight.
The Bard, in debt, whom Bailiffs ferret,
Despite his poetry and merit,
Stops in his quick retreat awhile,
And tries the long-forgotten smile;
E'en the pursuing Bum forgets
His business, and the man of Debts;
The one neglecting "Caption"—"Bail"—
The other "thoughts of gyves and Jail"—
So wondrous are the spells that bind
The noble and ignoble mind.
The Paviour halts in mid-grunt—stands
With rammer in his idle hands;
And quite refined, and at his ease,
Forgetting onions, bread, and cheese,
The hungry Drayman leaves his lunch,
To take a peep at Mister Punch.
Delightful thy effects to see,
Thou charm of age and infancy!
The old Man clears his rheumy eye,
The six months' Babe forgets to cry;
No passers by—all fondly gloat,
So welcome is thy cheering note,
Which time nor taste has ever changed;
And after every clime we've ranged,
Return to thee—our childhood's joy,
And, spite of age, still play the boy!
Yon pious Thing who walks by rule,
Unconscious laughs, and plays the fool,
And by his side the prim old Maid
Looks "welcome fun" and "who's afraid."
Behold, that happy ruddy face,
In which there seems no vacant place,
That could another joy impart,
For one laugh more would break his heart.
And, lo, behind! his sober Brother,
Striving in vain the laugh to smother.
That giggling Girl must burst outright,
For Punch has now possess'd her quite.
While She, who ran to Chemist's shop
For life or death—here finds a stop:
Forgets for whom—for what—she ran,
And leaves to Heaven the bleeding man!

The Parish Beadle, gilded calf,
Lays by his terror, joins the laugh,
Permits poor souls, without offence,
To sell their fruit and count their pence,
And, as by humour grown insane,
Allows the boys to touch his cane!
Poor little Sweep true comfort quaffs,
Ceases to cry—and loudly laughs.
See! what a wondrous powerful spell
Punch holds o'er Dustman and his bell;
And scolding Wife with clapper still—
The Landlord quits awhile his till,
While Pot-boy, busiest of the bunch,
Steals pence for self, and beer for Punch.
Look at that window, you may trace
At every pane a laughing face.
Yon graceful Girl and her smart Lover,
And in the story just above her,
The Housemaid, with her hair in papers,
All finding Punch a cure for vapours.
E'en the pale Dandy, fresh from France,
Throws on the group an eye askance;
Twirls his moustache, and seems to fear
That some gay friend may catch him here.
The Widowed wretch, who only fed,
On bitter thoughts and tear-wash'd bread,
Forgets her cares, and seems to smile
To see friend Punch her babe beguile.
Magician of the wounded heart,
Oh! there thy wonted aid impart:
Long be the merryman of our Isle,
And win the universal smile!

CONTENT

In some lone hamlet it were better far
  To live unknown amid Contentment's isle,
Than court the bauble of an air-blown star,
  Or barter honour for a prince's smile!
Hail! tranquil-brow'd Content, forth sylvan god,
  Who lov'st to sit beside some cottage fire,
Where the brown presence of the blazing clod
  Regales the aspect of the aged sire.
There, when the Winter's children, bleak and cold,
  Are through December's gloomy regions led;
The church-yard tale of sheeted ghost is told,

While fix'd attention dares not turn its head.
Or if the tale of ghost, or pigmy sprite,
  Is stripp'd by theme more cheerful of its power,
The song employs the early dim of night,
  Till village-curfew counts a later hour.
And oft the welcome neighbour loves to stop,
  To tell the market news, to laugh, and sing,
O'er the loved circling jug, whose old brown top
  Is wet with kisses from the florid ring!
There, whilst the cricket chirps its chimney song,
  Within some crumbling chink, with moss embrown'd,
The lighted stick diverts the infant throng,
  And fans are waved, and ribbands twirl'd around.
Entwine for me the wreath of rural mirth,
  And blast the murm'ring fiend, from chaos sent;
Then, while the house-dog snores upon the hearth,
  I'll sit, and hail thy sacred name, CONTENT!

EPITAPH

ON MATILDA

Sacred to Pity! is upraised this stone,
The humble tribute of a friend unknown;
To grant the beauteous wreck its hallow'd claim,
And add to misery's scroll another name.
Poor lost MATILDA! now in silence laid
Within the early grave thy sorrows made.
Sleep on!—his heart still holds thy image dear,
Who view'd, through life, thy errors with a tear;
Who ne'er with stoic apathy repress'd
The heartfelt sigh for loveliness distress'd.
That sigh for thee shall ne'er forget to heave;
'Tis all he now can give, or thou receive.
When last I saw thee in thy envied bloom,
That promised health and joy for years to come,
Methought the lily nature proudly gave,
Would never wither in th' untimely grave.
Ah, sad reverse! too soon the fated hour
Saw the dire tempest 'whelm th' expanding flower!
Then from thy tongue its music ceased to flow;
Thine eye forgot to gleam with aught but woe;
Peace fled thy breast; invincible despair
Usurp'd her seat, and struck his daggers there.
Did not the unpitying world thy sorrows fly?
And, ah! what then was left thee—but to die!

Yet not a friend beheld thy parting breath,
Or mingled solace with the pangs of death:
No priest proclaim'd the erring hour forgiven,
Or sooth'd thy spirit to its native heav'n:
But Heaven, more bounteous, bade the pilgrim come,
And hovering angels hail'd their sister home.
I, where the marble swells not, to rehearse
Thy hapless fate, inscribe my simple verse.
Thy tale, dear shade, my heart essays to tell;
Accept its offering, while it heaves—farewell!

TO —.

AN IMPROMPTU

O Sue! you certainly have been
  A little raking, roguish creature,
And in that face may still be seen
  Each laughing love's bewitching feature!
For thou hast stolen many a heart;
  And robb'd the sweetness of the rose;
Placed on that cheek, it doth impart
  More lovely tints—more fragrant blows!
Yes, thou art Nature's favourite child,
  Array'd in smiles, seducing, killing;
Did Joseph live, you'd drive him wild,
  And set his very soul a-thrilling!
A poet, much too poor to live,
  Too poor in this rich world to rove;
Too poor for aught but verse to give,
  But not, thank God, too poor to love!
Gives thee his little doggerel lay;—One
  truth I tell, in sorrow tell it:
I'm forced to give my verse away,
  Because, alas! I cannot sell it.
And should you with a critic's eye
  Proclaim me 'gainst the Muse a sinner,
Reflect, dear girl I that such as I,
  Six times a-week don't get a dinner.
And want of comfort, food, and wine,
  Will damp the genius, curb the spirit:
These wants I'll own are often mine;—
  But can't allow a want of merit.
For every stupid dog that drinks
  At poet's pond, nicknamed divine;
Say what he will, I know he thinks

That all he writes is wondrous fine!

Say, dark prow'd visitant! that o'er the brine
  Stalk'st proudly—heeding not what wind may blow,
What chart, what compass, shapes that course of thine,
  Whence didst thou come, and whither dost thou go?
Art thou a Monster born of sky and sea?
  Art thou a Pagod moving in thine ire?
Were I a Savage I must bend to thee,
  A Ghiber? I must own thee "God of fire."
The affrighted billows fly thy hissing rout,
  Thy wake is followed by turmoil and din,
Blackness and darkness track thy course without,
  And fire and groans and vapours strive within.
And they who cling about thee—who are they?
  And canst thou be that fabled boat, that waits
On the dark banks of Styx for souls? Oh, say!
  Let me not burst in ignorance—thy freight.
Thus spake I, wandering near the Brighton shore,
  Straining my very eye-balls from my Cab;
First came two "ten-horse" laughs—and then a roar,
  "Be off, queer Chap, or I'll soon stop your gab!"
Then swept she onward, breathing mist and cloud,
  While from my bosom this reflection broke;
Although I think the steam-boat something proud,
  Such lofty questions often end in smoke.
To all Grandiloquents a hint I deem it,
And whilst I live, I'll ever such esteem it.

SONNET

TO LYDIA, ON HER BIRTH-DAY

Bless'd be the hour that gave my LYDIA birth,
  The day be sacred 'mid each varying year;
How oft the name recals thy spotless worth,
  And joys departed, still to memory dear!
If matchless friendship, constancy, and love,
  Have power to charm, or one sad grief beguile,
'Tis thine the gloom of sorrow to remove,
  And on the tearful cheek imprint a smile.
May every after-season to thee bring

New joys, to cheer life's dark eventful way,
Till time shall close thee in his pond'rous wing,
  And angels waft thee to eternal day!
Loved friend, farewell! thy name this heart shall fill,
  Till memory sinks, and all its griefs are still!

TO SARAH, WHILE SINGING

Written at the Cottage of T. LEWIS, Esq. Woodbury Downs.

In the retirement of this lovely spot,
Sacred to friendship, industry, and worth,
To boundless hospitality and mirth,
Be ever peace and joy—all care forgot,
Save that which carest for a higher, holier, lot!
And thou, sweet girl, whose lovely modest mien,
Cheers the gay banquet with unconscious wiles,
Long mayest thou grace it with affection's smiles,
The vocal syren of this sylvan scene.
Warbling thy sweetest notes 'midst flowers and woodlands green.
Long be the social circle's grace and pride,
Of parents' hopes, the dearest and the best,
"The Dove of promise to this ark of rest:"
Who, when around the world's fierce billows ride,
Beareth the branch that speaks of the receding tide!

July, 1827

TO THADDEUS [1]

Farewell! loved youth, for still I hold thee dear,
  Though thou hast left me friendless and alone;
Still, still thy name recals the heartfelt tear,
  That hastes MATILDA to her wish'd-for home.
Why leave the wretch thy perfidy hath made,
  To journey cheerless through the world's wide waste?
Say, why so soon does all thy kindness fade,
  And doom me, thus, affliction's cup to taste?
Ungen'rous deed! to fly the faithful maid
  Who, for thy arms, abandon'd every friend;
Oh! cruel thought, that virtue, thus, betray'd,
  Should feel a pang that death alone can end.
Yet I'll not chide thee—And when hence you roam,
  Should my sad fate one tear of pity move,

Ah! then return! this bosom's still thy home,
　And all thy failings I'll repay with love.
Believe me, dear, at midnight, or at morn,
　In vain exhausted nature strives to rest,
Thy absence plants my pillow with a thorn,
　And bids me hope no more, on earth, for rest.
But if unkindly you refuse to hear,
　And from despair thy poor MATILDA have;
Ah! don't deny one tributary tear,
　To glisten sweetly o'er my early grave.
MATILDA.

[Footnote 1: The above lines were written at the request of a lady, and meant to describe the feelings of one "who loved not wisely, but too well."]

YOUTH AND AGE

I love the joyous thoughtless heart,
　The revels of the youthful mind,
'Ere sad experience points the dart,
　Which wounds so surely all mankind.
It glads me when the buoyant soul,
　Unconscious ranges, fancy free,
Draining the sweets of pleasure's bowl,
　And thinking all as blest as he.
Ah! me, yet sad it is to know,
　The many griefs the future brings,
That time must change that note to woe,
　Which now its merry carrol sings.
This "summer of the mind," alas!
　Must have its autumn—leafless, bare,
When all these pleasing phantoms pass,
　And end in winter, age, and care!
Such, such is life, the moral tells—
　The tempest, and its sunny smiles,
A warning voice the cheerful bells,
　The knell of death, our youth beguiles!

SENT FOR THE ALBUM OF THE REV. G— C—,

With a Drawing of the Head of an Eminent Artist

Dear Sir, you remember, when Herod of Jewry
Had given a ball, how a shocking old fury

Demanded, so bent was the vixen on slaughter.
The head of St. John at the hand of her daughter:
Now do not detest me, nor hold me in dread,
Because, like King Herod, I send you a head:
Not a saint's, by-the-bye, although taken from life,
But a head of my friend, by the hand of my wife.

WRITTEN UNDER AN ELEGANT DRAWING OF A DEAD CANARY BIRD

By Miss A.M. TURNER, Daughter of the Eminent Engraver

Death to the very life! not the closed eye,
  Not those small paralytic limbs alone,
But every feather tells so mournfully
  Thy fate, and that thy little life has flown.
Manhood forbids that I should weep, and yet
  Sadness comes o'er my spirit, and I stand
Gazing intensely, and with mute regret,
  Turn from the wonder of the artist's hand.
Exquisite artist! could I praise thee more
  Than by the silent admiration? no!
And now I try to praise I must deplore
  How feeble is the verse that tells thee so;
But thou art gaining for thyself a fame
Worthy thyself, thy sex, and thy dear father's name!

LINES SUGGESTED BY THE DEATH OF THE PRINCESS CHARLOTTE

Genius of England! wherefore to the earth
  Is thy plumed helm, thy peerless sceptre cast?
Thy courts of late with minstrelsy and mirth
  Rang jubilant, and dazzling pageants past;
Kings, heroes, martial triumphs, nuptial rites—
Now, like a cypress, shiver'd by the blast,
  Or mountain-cedar, which the lightning smites,
In dust and darkness sinks thy head declined,
  Thy tresses streaming wild on ocean's reckless wind.
Art thou not glorious?—In that night of storms,
  When He, in Power's supremacy elate,
  Gaul's fierce Usurper! fulminating fate,
  The Goth's barbaric tyranny restored,
And science, art, and all life's fairer forms,
  Sunk to the dark dominion of the sword:
Didst thou not, champion of insulted man!

Confront this stern Destroyer in his pride?
  Didst thou not crush him in the battle shock,
While recent victory shouted in his van,
  And shrunk the nations, shadow'd by his stride?
    Yea, chain him howling to yon desert rock,
  Where, thronging ghastly from uncounted graves,
  His victims murmur 'midst the groans of waves,
And mock his soul's despair, his deep blaspheming ban!
Nor erst, in Liberty's avenging day,
  When, launching lightnings in her wrath divine,
  She rose, and gave to never-dying fame,
Platæ, Marathon, Thermopylæ,
  Did each, did all, sublimer laurels twine
  Round Græcia's conquering brows, than Waterloo on thine!
Then, wherefore, Albion! terror-struck, subdued,
  Sitt'st thou, thy state foregone, thy banner furl'd?
What dire infliction shakes that fortitude,
  Which propt the falling fortunes of the world?—
Hush! hark! portentous, like a withering spell
  From lips unblest—strange sounds mine ear appal;
Now the dread omens more distinctly swell—
  That thrilling shriek from Claremont's royal hall,
The death-note peal'd from yon terrific bell,
  The deepening gale with lamentation swoln—
These, Albion! these, too eloquently tell,
  That from her radiant sphere, thy brightest star has fall'n!
And art thou gone?—graced vision of an hour!
  Daughter of Monarchs! gem of England's crown!
Thou loveliest lily! fair imperial flower!
  In beauty's vernal bloom to dust gone down;
Gone when, dispers'd each inauspicious cloud,
  In blissful sunshine 'gan thy hopes to glow:
From pain's fierce grasp, no refuge but the shroud,
  Destin'd a Mother's pangs, but not her joys, to know.
Lost excellence! what harp shall hymn thy worth,
  Nor wrong the theme? conspicuously in thee,
Beyond the blind pre-eminence of birth,
  Shone Nature in her own regality!
Coerced, thy Spirit smiled, sedate in pride,
  Fixt as the pine, while circling storms contend;
But, when in Life's serener duties tried,
  How sweetly did its gentle essence blend,
All-beauteous in the wife, the daughter, and the friend!
Not lull'd in langours, indolent and weak,
  Nor winged by pleasure, fled thy early hours;
But ceaseless vigils blanch'd thy virgin cheek,
  In silent Study's dim-sequester'd bowers:
Propitious there, to thy admiring mind,

With brow unveil'd, consenting Science came;
There Taste awoke her sympathies refined;
 There Genius, kindling his etherial flame,
Led thy young soul the Muse's heights to dare,
  And mount on Milton's wing, and breathe empyreal air!
But chiefly, conscious of thy promised throne,
  Intent to grace that destiny sublime;
Thou sought'st to make the historic page thine own,
  And win the treasures of recorded time;
The forms of polity, the springs of power,
  Exploring still with inexhausted zeal;
Still, the pole-star which led thy studious hour
  Through Thought's unfolding tracts—thy Country's weal!
While Fancy, radiant with unearthly charms,
  Thus breathed the whisper Wisdom sanctified:
"Eliza's, Anna's glories, arts, or arms,
  Beneath thy sway shall blaze revivified,
And still prolonged, and still augmenting, shine
Interminably bright in thy illustrious line!"
'Tis past—thy name, with every charm it bore,
Melts on our souls, like music heard no more,
The dying minstrel's last ecstatic strain,
Which mortal hand shall never wake again—
But, if, blest spirit! in thy shrine of light,
Life's visions rise to thy celestial sight;
If that bright sphere where raptured seraphs glow,
Permit communion with this world of woe;
And sore, if thus our fond affections deem,
Hope mocks us not, for Heaven inspires the dream—
Benignant shade! the beatific kiss
That seal'd thy welcome to the shores of bliss,
No holier joy instill'd, than then wilt feel
If thine the task thy kindred's woes to heal;
If hovering yet, with viewless ministry,
In scenes which Memory consecrates to thee,
Thou soothe with binding balm which grief endears,
A Sire's, a Husband's, and—a Mother's tears!—
Till Pity's self expire, a Nation's sighs,
Spontaneous incense! o'er thy tomb shall rise:
And, 'midst the dark vicissitudes that wait
Earth's balanced empires in the scales of Fate,
Be thou OUR angel-advocate the while,
And gleam, a guardian saint, around thy native isle!

Sung by Mr. PYNE.—Composed by Mr. ROOKE

Come away, come away, little fly!
  Don't disturb the sweet calm of lore's nest;
If you do, I protest you shall die,
  And your tomb be that beautiful breast.
Don't tickle the girl in her sleep,
  Don't cause so much beauty to sigh;
If she frown, half the graces will weep,
  If she weep, all the graces will die.
    Come away, little fly, &c.
Now she wakes! steal a kiss and be gone;
  Life is precious: away, little fly!
Should your rudeness provoke her to scorn,
  You'll meet death from the glance of her eye.
Were I ask'd by fair Chloe to say
  How I felt, as the flutterer I chid;
I should own, as I drove it away,
  I wish'd to be there in its stead!
    Come away, little fly, &c.

THE HEROES OF WATERLOO

Address, written for a Benefit, at a Provincial Theatre, for the Wounded Survivors, Families, and Relatives, of the Heroes of Waterloo

Once more Britannia sheathes her conqu'ring sword,
And Peace returns, by Victory restored;
Peace, that erewhile estranged, 'midst long alarms,
Scarce welcomed home, was ravish'd from our arms;
What time, fierce bounding from his broken chain,
Gaul's banish'd Despot re-aspired to reign;
Whilst at his call, prompt minions of his breath,
Round his dire throne rush'd Havoc, Spoil, and Death;
With wonted pomp his baleful ensign blazed,
And Europe shrunk, and shudder'd as she gazed.
Insulted Liberty her tocsin rung;
Again Britannia to the combat sprung:
Star of the Nations! her auspicious form
Led on their march, and foremost braved the storm.
Pent-in its clouds, ere yet the tempest flash'd,
Ere peal on peal the mingling thunder crash'd;
While Fate hung dubious o'er the marshall'd powers,
What anxious fears, what trembling hopes, were ours!
For never yet from Gallia's confines came
War's fell eruption with so fierce a flame:

She sent a Chief, matur'd in martial strife,
Who fought for fame, for empire, and for life;
Whose Host had sworn, deep-stung with recent shame,
To satiate vengeance, and retrieve their fame!
Each furious impulse, each hot throb, was there,
That spurs Ambition, or inflames Despair.
Then Britain fix'd on her Unconquer'd Son,
Her eye, her hope—immortal WELLINGTON!
He, skill'd to crash, with one collective blow
Sustain'd sedate the fierce assaulting foe.
How stood his squadrons like the steadfast rock,
Frowning on Ocean's ineffectual shock!
Till forward summon'd to the fierce attack,
They give to Gaul his furious onset back;
Swift on its prey each fiery legion springs,
As when Heaven's ire the vollied lightning wings!
Then Gallia's blood in expiation stream'd,
Then trembling Europe saw her fate redeem'd;
And England, radiant in her triumph past,
Beheld them all transcended in the last:
Yes, raptured Britons blest the gale that blew
The tidings home—the tale of Waterloo!
But, oh! while joy tumultuous hail'd the day,
Cold on the plain what gallant victims lay!
Deaf to the triumph of their sacred cause,
Deaf to their country's shout, the world's applause!
Rear high the column, bid the marble breathe,
Pour soft the verse, and twine the laureate wreath;
From year to year let musing Memory shed
Her tenderest tears, to grace the glorious dead.
'Tis ours with grateful ardour to sustain
The wounded veteran on his bed of pain;
To soothe the widow, sunk in anguish deep,
Whose orphan weeps to see its mother weep.
Oh! when, outstretch'd on that triumphant field,
The prostrate Warrior felt his labours seal'd;
Felt, 'midst the shout of Victory pealing round,
Life's eddying stream fast welling from his wound;
Perchance Affection bade her visions rise—
Wife, children, floated o'er his closing eyes:
For them alone he heaved the bitter sigh;
Yet for his country glorying thus to die!
To her bequeath'd them with his parting breath,
And sunk serene in unregretted death.—
To no cold ear was that appeal prefer'd;
With glowing bosom grateful England heard;
With liberal hand she pours the prompt relief,
Soothes the sick head, and wipes the tear of grief.

Our humble efforts consecrate, to-night,
To this great cause, our small but willing mite.
Bright are the wreaths the warrior's urn which grace,
And bless'd the bounty that protects his race!
Thus warm'd, thus waken'd, with congenial fire,
Each hero's son shall emulate his sire;
From age to age prolong the glorious line,
And guard their country with a shield divine!

THE NIGHT-BLOWING CEREUS

Can it be true, so fragrant and so fair,
　To give thy perfumes to the dews of night?
Can aught so beautiful, despise the glare,
　And fade, and sicken in the morning light?
Yes! peerless flower, the Heavens alone exhale
　Thy fragrance, while the glittering stars attest,
And incense wafted by the midnight gale,
　Untainted rises from thy spotless breast.
How like that Faith whose nature is apart
　From human gaze, to love and work unseen,
Which gives to God an undivided heart,
　In sorrow steadfast, and in joy serene;
That night-flower of the soul, whose fragrant power
Breathes on the darkness of the closing hour!

1827; OR, THE POET'S LAST POEM

Ye Bards in all your thousand dens,
Great souls with fewer pence than pens,
Sublime adorers of Apollo,
With folios full, and purses hollow;
Whose very souls with rapture glisten,
When you can find a fool to listen;
Who, if a debt were paid by pun,
Would never be completely done.
Ye bright inhabitants of garrets,
Whose dreams are rich in ports and clarets,
Who, in your lofty paradise,
See aldermanic banquets rise—
And though the duns around you troop,
Still float in seas of turtle soup.
I here forsake the tuneful trade,
Where none but lordlings now are paid,

Or where some northern rogue sits puling,
(The curse of universal schooling)—
A ploughman to his country lost,
An author to his printer's cost—
A slave to every man who'll buy him,
A knave to every man who'll try him—
Yet let him take the pen, at once
The laurel gathers round his sconce!
On every subject superseded,
My favorite topics all invaded,
I scarcely dip my pen in praise,
When fifty bardlings grasp my bays;
Or let me touch a drop of satire,
(I once knew something of the matter),
Just fifty bardlings take the trouble,
To be my tuneful worship's double.
Fine similies that nothing fit,
Joe Miller's, that must pass for wit;
The dull, dry, brain-besieging jokes,
The humour that no laugh provokes—
The nameless, worthless, witless rancours,
The rage that souls of scribblers cankers—
(Administer'd in gall go thick,
It makes even Sunday critic's sick!)
Disgust my passion, fill my place,
And snatch my prize before my face.
If then I take the "brilliant" pen.
And "scorning measures" talk of men—
There Luttrel steps 'twixt me and fame—
So like, egad, we're just the same;
I never half squeeze out a thought,
But jumps its fellow on the spot—
My tenderest dreams, my fondest touch,
Are victims to his ready clutch;
The whirling waltz, the gay costume,
The porcelain tooth, the gallic bloom;
The vapid smiles, the lisping loves
Of turtles (never meant for doves)—
The dreary stuff that fills the ears,
Where all the orators are peers—
The hides reveal'd through ball-room dresses,
Where all the parties are peer-esses;
The dulness of the toujours gai,
The yawning night, the sleepy day,
The visages of cheese and chalk,
The drowsy, dreamy, languid talk;
The fifty other horrid things,
That strip old Time of both his wings!

There's not a topic of them all
But comes, hey presto! at his call.
Or when I turn my pen to love,
A theme that fits me like my glove,
A pang I've borne these twenty years
With ten-times twenty several dears,
Each glance a dart, each smile a quiver,
Stinging their bard from lungs to liver—
To work my ruin, or my cure,
Up starts thy pen, Anacreon Moore!
In vain I pour my shower of roses,
On which the matchless fair one dozes,
And plant around her conch the graces,
While jealous Venus breaks her laces,
To see a younger face promoted,
To see her own old face out-voted;
And myrtle branches twisting o'er her,
Bow down, each turn'd a true adorer.
Up starts the Irish Bard—in vain
I write, 'tis all against the grain:
In vain I talk of smiles or sighs,
The girls all have him in their eyes;
And not a soul—mamma, or miss—
But vows he's the sole Bard of Bliss!
Since first I dipp'd in the romantic,
A hundred thousand have run frantic—
There's not a hideous highland spot,
(Long fallowed to the core by Scott)—
No rill, through rack and thistle dribbling,
But has its deadlier crop of scribbling.
Each fen, and flat, and flood, and fell,
Gives birth to verses by the ell—
There Wordsworth, for his muse's sallies,
Claims all the ponds, the lanes, and alleys—
There Coleridge swears none else shall tune
A bag-pipe to the list'ning moon;
On come in clouds the scribbling columns,
Each prowling for his next three volumes.
I scorn the rascal tribe, and spurn all
The yearly, monthly, and diurnal.
I write the finest things that ever
Made duchess fond, or marquiss clever—
(Although I'd rather half turn Turk,
The thing's such monstrous up-hill work).
My ton's the very cream of fashion,
My passion the sublimest passion,
My rage satanic, love the same,
Of all blue flames, the bluest flame—

My piety perpetual matins,
A quaker propp'd on double pattens;
My lovely girls the most precocious,
My beaus delightfully atrocious!
Yet scarcely have I play'd my card,
When up comes politician Ward,
Before my face he trumps my trump,
Sweeps off my honours in the lump,
And never asking my permission,
Talks sermons to the third edition.
Or Boulogne, Highway Byeway, Grattan,
(The Pyrenees begin to flatten,
A feast denied to storm and shower,
The pen's the wonder-working power);
Or Smith, the master of "Addresses,"
Carves history out in modern messes:—
Tells how gay Charles cook'd up his collops,
How fleeced his friends, how paid his trollops—
How pledged his soul, and pawn'd his oath,
'Till none would give a straw for both;
And touching paupers for the Evil,
Touch'd England half way to the devil
Or Hook, picks up my favorite hits,
For when was friendship between wits?
Or Lyster, doubly dandyfied,
Fidgets his donkey by my side;
Or Bulwer rambles back from Greece,
Woolgathering from the Golden fleece—
Or forty volumes, piping hot,
Come blazing from volcano Scott;
When pens like their's play all my game.
The tasteless world must bear the blame.
I had a budget, full of fan,
But here again, I'm lost, undone!
I'm so forestall'd—that faith, I could
Half quarrel with—my lively Hood:
For odd it is, my "Oddities,"
Are even all the same with his;
Would Sherwood (him of Paternoster),
Assist my pilferings to foster,
I'd turn free-booter—nay, I would
E'en play the part of robbing Hood—
But brother Wits should never quarrel,
Nor try to "pluck each other's laurel,"
And tho' my income's scarce enough
To find friend Petersham with snuff,
Here's peace to all! and kind regards!
And Brother Hood among the Bards.

So all, friends, countrymen, and lovers,
With one, or one and twenty covers,
Farewell to all;—my glories past,
I pen my lay, my sweetest, last!
Another Phoenix, build my nest
Of spices, Phoebus' very best,
Concentrating in these gay pages,
Wit, worth the wit of all the stages;
Love, tender as the midnight talk,
In softest summer's midnight walk,
With leave to all earth's fools to spurn 'em,
Nay (if they first will buy) to burn 'em.

TO THE REVIEWERS

Oh! ye, enthroned in presidential awe,
To give the song-smit generation law;
Who wield Apollo's delegated rod,
And shake Parnassus with your sovereign nod;
A pensive Pilgrim, worn with base turmoils,
Plebeian cares, and mercenary toils,
Implores your pity, while with footsteps rude,
He dares within the mountain's pale intrude;
For, oh! enchantment through its empire dwells.
And rules the spirit with Lethëan spells;
By hands unseen aërial harps are hung,
And Spring, like Hebe, ever fair and young,
On her broad bosom rears the laughing Loves,
And breathes bland incense through the warbling groves;
Spontaneous, bids unfading blossoms blow,
And nectar'd streams mellifluously flow.
There, while the Muses wanton unconfined,
And wreaths resplendent round their temples bind,
'Tis yours to strew their steps with votive flowers;
To watch them slumbering 'midst the blissful bowers;
To guard the shades that hide their sacred charms;
And shield their beauties from unhallow'd arms!
Oh! may their suppliant steal a passing kiss?
Alas! he pants not for superior bliss;
Thrice-bless'd his virgin modesty shall be
To snatch an evanescent ecstacy!
The fierce extremes of superhuman love,
For his frail sense too exquisite might prove;
He turns, all blushing, from th' Aönian shade,
To humbler raptures with a mortal maid.
I know 'tis yours, when unscholastic wights

Unloose their fancies in presumptuous flights,
Awaked to vengeance, on such flights to frown,
Clip the wing'd horse, and roll his rider down.
But, if empower'd to strike th' immortal lyre,
The ardent vot'ry glows with genuine fire,
'Tis yours, while care recoils, and envy flies,
Subdued by his resistless energies,
'Tis yours to bid Piërian fountains flow,
And toast his name in Wit's seraglio;
To bind his brows with amaranthine bays,
And bless, with beef and beer, his mundane days!
Alas! nor beef, nor beer, nor bays, are mine,
If by your looks my doom I may divine,
Ye frown so dreadful, and ye swell so big,
Your fateful arms, the goose-quill, and the wig:
The wig, with wisdom's somb'rous seal impress'd,
Mysterious terrors, grim portents, invest;
And shame and honour on the goose-quill perch,
Like doves and ravens on a country church.
As some raw 'Squire, by rustic nymphs admired,
Of vulgar charms, and easy conquests tired,
Resolves new scenes and nobler flights to dare,
Nor "waste his sweetness in the desert air,"
To town repairs, some famed assembly seeks,
With red importance blust'ring in his cheeks;
But when, electric on th' astonish'd wight
Burst the full floods of music and of light,
While levell'd mirrors multiply the rows
Of radiant beauties, and accomplish'd beaus,
At once confounded into sober sense,
He feels his pristine insignificance:
And blinking, blund'ring, from the general quiz
Retreats, "to ponder on the thing he is."
By pride inflated, and by praise allured,
Small Authors thus strut forth, and thus get cured;
But, Critics, hear I an angel pleads for me,
That tongueless, ten-tongued cherub, Modesty.
Sirs! if you damn me, you'll resemble those
That flay'd the Traveller who had lost his clothes;
Are there not foes enough to do my books?
Relentless trunk-makers and pastry-cooks?
Acknowledge not those barbarous allies,
The wooden box-men, and the men of pies:
For Heav'n's sake, let it ne'er be understood
That you, great Censors! coalesce with wood;
Nor let your actions contradict your looks,
That tell the world you ne'er colleague with cooks.
But, if the blithe Muse will indulge a smile,

Why scowls thy brow, O Bookseller! the while?
Thy sunk eyes glisten through eclipsing fears,
Fill'd, like Cassandra's, with prophetic tears:
With such a visage, withering, woe-begone,
Shrinks the pale poet from the damning dun.
Come, let us teach each other's tears to flow,
Like fasting bards, in fellowship of woe,
When the coy Muse puts on coquettish airs,
Nor deigns one line to their voracious prayers!
Thy spirit, groaning like th' encumber'd block
Which bears my works, deplores them as dead stock.
Doom'd by these undiscriminating times
To endless sleep, with Delia Cruscan rhymes;
Yes, Critics whisper thee, litigious wretches!
Oblivion's hand shall finish all my sketches.
But see, my soul, such bug-bears has repell'd
With magnanimity unparallel'd!
Take up the volume, every care dismiss,
And smile, gruff Gorgon! while I tell thee this:
Not one shall lie neglected on the shelf,
All shall be sold—I'll buy them in myself!

Thomas Gent – A Concise Bibliography

Gent is known to have published more than sixty works, among those he authored are:

God's judgments shewn unto mankind. Being a true and sorrowful relation of the sufferings of the city of Marseilles in France (1720)
The forsaken lover's letter to his former sweetheart (1722)
Divine entertainments: or, penitential desires, sighs, and groans of the wounded soul (1724)
The Antient and Modern History of the famous City of York (1730)
The History of the Loyal Town of Rippon (1733)
Miscellanae curiosae: or entertainments for the ingenious of both sexes (1733)
The pattern of piety: or, Tryals of Patience. Being The Most Faithful Spiritual Songs of the Life and Death of the once Afflicted Job (1734)
Annales Regioduni Hullini: Or, The History of the Royal and Beautiful Town of Kingston-upon-Hull (1869)
Pater patriae: being, an elegiac pastoral dialogue (1738)
Historia Compendiosa Anglicana: Or, A Compendious and Delightful History of England ... A succinct History of ROME, from its Foundation by Romulus 'till the Fall of K. Tarquin.. An Appendix, relating to York. A further Historical Account of Pontefract (1741)
Volume 1: Historia Compendiosa Anglicana; Book 2; Book 3; Book 4; Book 5; A Comprehensive dissertation on the Ancient and Present State of Pontefract..
Volume 2: Historia Compendiola Romana; Book 6; Book 7; Book 8; Book 9; Addenda; Appendix; Index, errata
British piety display'd in the glorious life, suffering, and death of the blessed St. Winefred (1742)
The Holy Life and Death of St. Winefred and other Religious Persons in Five Parts (1742)

The History of the Life and Miracles of our Blessed Saviour Jesus Christ from His Birth to His Cruxifixion. As also the lives, sufferings and death of the Evangelists and Apostles
Piety Display'd in the Holy Life and Death of the Antient and Celebrated St. Robert, Hermit, at Knaresborough. (2 ed.)
The most delectable, scriptural, and pious history of the famous great easter window ... in St. Peter's Cathedral, York (1762)
The pious and poetical works. 11 parts (1734–72)
The Contingencies, Vicissitdues or Changes of this transitory Life..., 1761, transcript with notes of a performed prologue
Poetical pieces by Thomas Gent (1772)
Set forth the unhappy Birth, wicked Life, and miserable End of that deceitful Apostle, Judas Iscariot (1772)

Autobiography

Life of Mr. Thomas Gent, Printer of York; written by himself (1832)

www.ingramcontent.com/pod-product-compliance
Lightning Source LLC
Chambersburg PA
CBHW021939040426
42448CB00008B/1145